Claudette Colvin

Forgotten Mother
of the
Civil Rights Movement

Also by this author

Nat Turner's Holy War To Destroy Slavery
America's Female Buffalo Soldier: Cathy Williams
Miller Cornfield at Antietam
Pickett's Charge
Death at the Little Bighorn
Barksdale's Charge
Storming Little Round Top
Exodus From The Alamo
Emily D. West and the "Yellow Rose of Texas" Myth
The South's Finest
George Washington's Surprise Attack
How The Irish Won The American Revolution
Why Custer Was Never Warned
The Alamo's Forgotten Defenders
Irish Confederates
God Help The Irish!
Burnside's Bridge
The Final Fury
Westerners In Gray
Alexander Hamilton's Revolution
The Confederacy's Fighting Chaplain
Cubans In The Confederacy
Forgotten Stonewall of the West
From Auction Block To Glory
The Important Role of the Irish in the American Revolution
The 1862 Plot to Kidnap Jefferson Davis.
Anne Bonny: The Infamous Female Pirate
America's Forgotten First War for Slavery and Genesis of The Alamo
For Honor, Country, and God: Los Niños Héroes
Targeting Abraham: The Forgotten 1865 Plot To Assassinate Lincoln
A New Look at the Buffalo Soldier Experience in Wartime Vol I:
Corporal David Fagen's Metamorphosis and Odyssey
Nanny's War to Destroy Slavery
The Irish at Gettysburg
Blacks in Gray Uniforms
Glory At Fort Wagner: The 54th Massachusetts Vol I
Roll of Honor and the Price of Glory: The 54th Massachusetts Vol II
Forgotten Contributions of "Little Africa" Soldiers at Fort Wagner:
The 54th Massachusetts Vol III

Claudette Colvin

Forgotten Mother
of the
Civil Rights Movement

Phillip Thomas Tucker, Ph.D.

Copyright © 2020 Phillip Thomas Tucker

All rights reserved, including the right to reproduce this book, or portions thereof in any form. No part of this text may be reproduced, transmitted, downloaded, decompiled, reverse engineered, or stored, in any form or introduced into any information storage and retrieval system, in any form or by any means, whether electronic or mechanical without the express written permission of the author.

The views expressed in this work are solely those of the author and do not necessarily reflect the views of the publisher, and the publisher hereby disclaims any responsibility for them.

ISBN: 9798644051748

PublishNation LLC
www.publishnation.net

Contents

Introduction	1
Chapter I: Dark Days for African Americans	19
Chapter II: The Value of Black History Month 1955 and the Forgotten Young Woman that Gave Birth to the Civil Rights Movement	44
Chapter III: A Rendezvous With Destiny	67
Epilogue	113
About the Author	116
Bibliography	117

Introduction

On March 2, 1955, a courageous black teenager of Montgomery, Alabama, named Claudette Colvin took a giant step forward for not only African American rights but also human rights. On her own, she provided the first spark that resulted in the Civil Rights Movement by refusing to surrender her seat to a white woman like the strict and oppressive segregation laws of the city and state required.

Most importantly, Claudette eventually inspired Rosa Parks to shortly play a comparable defiant role on a segregated bus that officially—and according to the history books—led to the famous Montgomery Bus Boycott, the Civil Rights Movement, and the dramatic rise of Dr. Martin Luther King to prominence.

These were all key developments of a remarkable social movement that eventually changed the world, especially the lives of millions of African Americans long mired in oppression. Most importantly for the true historical record, Claudette Colvin was a forgotten founder of the Civil Rights Movement. She became an early pioneer and inspirational player of the earth-shaking social movement and more so than Rosa Parks or Dr. King in the very beginning before they became national figures.

Only two years after the Korean War's end and in the same year that Senator John Fitzgerald Kennedy wrote—the book was officially released on January 1, 1956 but pre-publication copies were circulated far and wide and then became a national best seller—his first book, Claudette made her defiant stand for equality and freedom. Most important, Colvin's refusal to relinquish her seat to an older white woman on a Montgomery bus at age fifteen on Wednesday March 2, 1955 eventually helped to change the world.

As planned by Kennedy's savvy political campaign managers, this widely-acclaimed book helped to put the young Massachusetts senator on the path to the presidency in 1960. Although critics have long charged that this popular book was ghostwritten by others, Kennedy's *Profiles in Courage* won the Pulitzer Prize in 1957.

Most of all and as planned by the powerful Kennedy political machine of the northeast which was supported by wealthy backers, especially his rich father, Joseph P. Kennedy, Senior, this popular book introduced the American public to the young Massachusetts senator, who was destined to become America's first Roman Catholic president in only five years. Unlike Claudette Colvin who hailed from the poorest black neighborhood (King Hill) of Montgomery, Kennedy hailed from one of the richest and powerful families in America.

However, Kennedy's *Profiles in Courage* had its serious limitations because it was so narrowly focused, especially in terms of gender, race, and class. It was a book devoted to the moral courage and integrity demonstrated by political elites (privileged United States Senators in this case) and written about upper class members of American society over an extended period.

In 1964, the memorial edition of *Profiles in Courage* was released with a lengthy foreword and tribute to the recently assassinated president, who had been felled by assassin's bullets on November 22, 1963 in the streets of Dallas, Texas. This foreword was written by his admiring younger brother, Robert F. Kennedy.

In the foreword's first sentence to introduce readers to this popular book, Robert F. Kennedy wrote how: "Courage is the virtue that President Kennedy most admired [and] He sought out those people who had demonstrated in some way . . . that they had courage, that they would stand you, that they could be counted on."

Of course, these are noble and powerful words about personal heroics that still apply to this day, because admirable displays of courage in times of crisis and decisive situations are still the most revered qualities of the American people, even during America's unheroic and cynical age of today. But, ironically, such moral courage that Kennedy emphasized in his book over the years has today become the rarest and most extinct of qualities in today's world of self-serving politics, especially in Washington, D.C.

At a later point in this memorial edition's foreword that was written partly because of renewed interest among the grieving public after President Kennedy's assassination that once again ensured that the book became a best seller, brother Robert emphasized how the book "tells the stories of men who in their own time recognized what needed to be done—and did it . . . If there is a lesson from the lives of the men John Kennedy depicts in this book, if there is a lesson from his life and from his death, it is that in this world of ours none of us can afford to be lookers on, the critics standing on the sidelines."

In the first line of his popular book, Senator John Fitzgerald Kennedy wrote how: "This is a book about the most admirable of human virtues—courage [and contains] the stories of the pressures experienced by eight United States Senators and the grace with which they endured them—the risks to their careers, the unpopularity of their courses, the defamation of their characters . . . ."

Of course, such a special focus on courage among United States Senators was most commendable and Kennedy's book caused a sensational among America's reading public both before and after his tragic death from the killer's bullets in Dallas. However and as noted, Kennedy's book was extremely limited in its overall scope and perspective to say the least. After all, it had been written primarily to boast the political career of a young Massachusetts senator with ambitions of reaching the executive office at the White House, which he eventually accomplished on January 20, 1961.

After all, any mention of a black person, especially an African American woman who was a member of the most vulnerable, abused, and despised race in America and permanently mired at the lowest rung of the social order, would have lost him votes for the presidency. Therefore, all eight subjects of *Profiles in Courage* were white male senators of the ruling elite, who stood tall in the halls of Congress in Washington, D.C., because of their political power and displays of political courage.

Therefore, for the most part, Kennedy's revered work was very much a political book written primarily for political reasons that were mostly selfishly focused, especially in regard to the pursuit of the presidency. Each of this slim book's eight chapters were devoted to the demonstrated personal integrity of eight United States senators. Clearly, the book was written in part because the ambitious Kennedy was attempting to publicity.

Therefore and as mentioned, Kennedy's book has provided very limited and carefully-chosen examples of moral courage because of the focus on not only just privileged senators, but also just white males, who enjoyed positions of power. Including both obscure and well-known individuals, these figures chosen by Kennedy were senators from the nineteenth century to the twentieth century and from John Quincy Adams to Robert A. Taft.

Of course at this time and as noted, no thought existed in Kennedy's or any other senator's and publisher's mind of including any member of the most helpless and discriminated race and sex in America in the pages of this popular book. Consequently, no person of color or of the female sex became subjects in this book, which was clearly written for a white audience, especially future voters, at time when African Americans, including Claudette Colvin, were still struggling to win the most basic equality and rights.

But contrary to what was written in Kennedy's book, the true and best examples of true moral courage have not been forthcoming in the annals of American history from wealthy, upper class, and aristocratic white politicians of the privileged elite. Instead, the best example of true moral courage under the most extreme and disadvantageous circumstances in America have come from members of the lowest order of American society, because they faced the greatest odds that seemed insurmountable unlike the white senators of Kennedy's book, African Americans.

After all, during the 1950s in the period of Jim Crow discrimination and racism that was deeply-enshrined in Alabama's city and state laws, it was African American people who faced the greatest odds and risked the highest cost—physical violence and even death, usually by mob lynching—for demonstrating moral courage by standing up against racism, white authority, and discriminatory segregation laws.

Clearly, this deadly situation was a most daunting challenge of all for African Americans in America, because protesting blacks faced an institutionalized racism of a strict American Apartheid system. And this racist system was backed up by laws, the courts, the police, and informal citizen enforcers like the ever-violent Ku Klux Klan, which included well-armed police officers and even military members, across the South, when Kennedy's book was released.

As could be expected under such risky circumstances and given America's dismal racial realities of an Apartheid system, Kennedy's book made no mention of the almost unimaginable kind of black moral courage that made the far less risky and far more tame examples of moral courage displayed by these chosen white senators pale considerably by comparison to Claudette Colvin, because, in fact, there was actually no comparison at all.

At this time during an especially dark chapter of American history and without doubt, what took the greatest amount of moral courage was for blacks to boldly face the odds during the protests and dissent actions against the greatest racial injustices of all in America, especially black women.

Indeed, it was African American women, holding the lowest order in both American society and black society, who faced the greatest odds and highest risks in protesting against racial injustices, because of their gender to significantly dwarf the traditional societal pressures and career trials faced by the white members of the privileged class of Kennedy's revered white senators.

Therefore, actuality and beyond all doubt, the heroic example of the history-minded Montgomery, Alabama, teenager named Claudette Colvin can stand entirely on its own as a true *Profiles in Courage*. She defied the white Apartheid system and bravely stood up alone without supporters and by herself after her friends had left her all alone on the segregated Montgomery bus, which was governed by discriminatory city and state Jim Crow laws.

By herself, Claudette not only defied an angry white bus driver, but also an irate transit officer and then two of Montgomery's police officers by boldly standing up against America's own Apartheid system of Jim Crow: an audacious act which was unimaginable in 1955 Montgomery, especially for a fifteen-year-old high school student.

What Claudette demonstrated was the very epitome and essence of a true exhibition of courage and moral integrity on multiple levels and far more than anything revealed in the pages of Kennedy's highly-acclaimed book, which swept the nation at the same time Claudette made her defiant stand. The odds against Colvin were nothing short of insurmountable on every level to the point of having been something almost unimaginable to Americans today and especially someone from a wealthy, powerful family of the upper class elite, Senator Kennedy, in 1955.

Most prophetically, in the foreword of the best-selling memorial edition of *Profiles in Courage*, Robert Kennedy wrote how: "only the very courageous will be able to keep alive the spirit of individualism and dissent which gave birth to this nation . . . ." These words are the very definition of Claudette Colvin and what she achieved on March 2, 1955 in the name of equal rights and freedom for all.

In striking contrast to the subjects of Kennedy's book, the subject of this current book by this current author gave a dramatic birth to a social movement of America's most oppressed people that finally forced the United States to legally abolish its Apartheid system and live up to its most lofty egalitarian principles, which were first expressed in the Declaration of Independence.

Symbolically, this historic document that changed the world had been issued by the founding fathers from Independence Hall in Philadelphia, Pennsylvania, on July 4, 1776 during the people's revolution, which began with massive protest movements of the common people against England's abusive autocratic and dictatorial control of the colonies, especially the punitive Coercive Acts.

Claudette Colvin was part of a distinguished protest tradition of America. Colonial America's first protests were directed against King George III and his ministers, which eventually led to the war that resulted in the winning of independence. Centered in Boston, Massachusetts, America's foremost colonial revolutionaries were accomplished men of means, including upper class members and some of the richest men in America, from George Washington to John Hancock.

In contrast, Colvin, who hailed from one of Montgomery's poorest black neighborhoods, similarly sparked a distinctive people's movement on her own that was the antithesis of the colonists' well-organized mass protests, including colonial assemblies, the first Continental Congress, and the mass participation of the American people. Even more in the beginning, Claudette had no supporters or helpful network to back her like Rosa Parks, when she decided to make her solitary act of defiance on a segregated Montgomery bus on Wednesday March 2, 1955.

Indeed, in the end and compared to Kennedy's elitist white subjects of his Pulitzer Prize-winning book, the greater degree of moral courage and sheer heroism demonstrated by this remarkable young, high school student, after she had been oppressed by Jim Crow discrimination for her entire life since her birth on September 5, 1939, gave new meaning from a famous Dante quote: "the hottest places in Hell are reserved for those who, in a time of great moral crisis, maintain their neutrality"—Claudette's unfortunate situation, to her ever-lasting disgust, because the black adults of Montgomery had been so thoroughly intimated that they had accepted Alabama's harsh racial realities.

And, most importantly, the dramatic story of Claudette Colvin has demonstrated that doing the right thing and following the dictates of one's moral conscience by a single person, regardless of age, sex, or color, has continued to remain all-important to this day. What should not be forgotten, as Claudette proved in full, was that a single moral act of brave defiance by a determined individual following their conscience can help to change the world for the better: a timeless lesson that still applies to this day in the twenty-first century just like in 1955.

In early March 1955, not only the entire black population, especially the long-oppressed older generation, of Montgomery and much of the Deep South maintained a shameless "neutrality" by taking no protest action and only complaining about the seemingly endless Jim Crow injustices. By accepting all of the injustices, African Americans were doing nothing about the stifling oppression because they had learned from past experiences that nothing meaningful could be accomplished against such a powerful white establishment that seemed unchallengeable in every way because of the inevitable violent backlash.

Even more, in Montgomery—the most Southern of cities— and much like the rest of the Deep South, the core spiritual tenets of Christianity had been completely turned upside down by the Jim Crow laws of the white privileged class to entrench their own power to the ever-lasting disgust of a devout Claudette, who internalized the shame and disgrace. Praying as hard as she studied and excelled in high school, especially in black history, Claudette saw how the dictates and laws of God had been completely perverted in Montgomery by the racial injustices of Jim Crow like nowhere else in America.

Claudette, who was supremely religious and believed that "God loved everyone" <u>equally</u>, decided to stand-up to the autocratic and racist rules of white Americans, because she knew that they had turned their backs on their own religious faith and the very meaning of Christianity to keep the weight of Jim Crow on the throat of an oppressed minority of second class citizens like the infamous Apartheid system of South Africa.

But, despite only a teenager and nine months before Rosa Parks' defiant actions on another segregated Montgomery bus transformed her into a cherished icon of the Civil Rights Movement, which has often been romanticized and mythologized to distort some actual facts, only one person in

Montgomery acted on their own and boldly stood-up for themselves and their people in early March 1955.

This situation that Claudette Colvin found herself was entirely unlike Parks, who enjoyed the complete and extensive support of the National Association for the Advancement of Colored People (NAACP) and the protest movement's top leaders in not only Montgomery, but also in Alabama.

Without advice, coaching, or guidance of any kind or from anyone else, Claudette simply made-up her mind and decided that it was now time to take a defiant stand against racism and injustice, which shortly brought cheers and admiration from both the younger and older generation of African Americas not only in Montgomery, but also across the South: the most forgotten and overlooked vital spark that resulted in the birth of the famous Montgomery Bus Boycott, which then opened the door to greater developments and change of a most significant nature.

Indeed, Claudette Colvin's actions were in fact the true beginning of the Civil Rights Movement that included the rise of a gifted, young minister named Dr. Martin Luther King and other Civil Rights leaders, who now decided that it was time to fight back like Claudette made her defiant stand against Jim Crow: the dramatic events that changed not only America, but also the world.

At the time, not even Claudette fully realized the importance of what she had done on March 2, 1955 by defying white abusive authority and racist segregation laws until her beloved pastor, Reverend H. H. Johnson, stunned her in private by admitting: "Claudette, I am so proud of you. Everyone prays for freedom [and] I think you just brought the revolution to Montgomery."

In the end, the good reverend's words of praise were no exaggeration or hyperbole. Claudette had indeed started a true people's revolution for justice in Montgomery, while firing a symbolic shot across the bow of Jim Crow. This shot began a movement, and, therefore, was heard across the South like the firing of the Massachusetts Minute-Men, who had stood firm and fought the British regulars for their rights and liberties on April 19, 1775 to start the American Revolution.

Unfortunately, Claudette Colvin had been largely forgotten today because her early contributions became an ignored memory and legacy, after they—like Claudette herself—were cast into the shadows by Civil Rights icon Rosa Parks of Montgomery and the Civil Rights Movement in upcoming years.

Unlike Claudette, Parks, a respected, longtime member of the NAACP, was handpicked by top black leadership to become the symbol of new boycott movement in Montgomery nine months later when arrested for refusing to relinquish her seat a city bus to a white person on December 1, 1955. A combination of pressing and complex factors, ordained by a cruel fate for her legacy and memory at no fault of her own, was destined to regulate Claudette to a deliberately-orchestrated obscurity, which was entirely undeserved on every level.

As dictated by the actions of the Civil Rights Movement leaders and sadly for her distinguished early legacy, Claudette was simply cast into a dark obscurity because she was considered too young, too black, too poor, too emotional, too immature, too pregnant, too uncontrollable, no nuclear family, and too feisty in the view of the older generation of leaders. For example, at age forty-two and more than 25 years older than Claudette, Parks could have been not only Colvin's mother but also her grandmother.

In 1955, Claudette was only a typical teenager who loved to dance and music like her friends and the other students at Booker T. Washington High School in Montgomery. However, it was true that Claudette also became a feisty rebel of strong opinions and a religiously-inspired conscience in a remarkable metamorphosis, because of the longtime Jim Crow abuses, which had made black life so miserable and endlessly humiliating. She hated racial injustice and Jim Crow with a passion, long before she had been arrested for having violated the segregation laws on March 2, 1955.

From the beginning and almost like savvy publicists working on Madison Avenue, top black leaders, including Dr. Martin Luther King, knew that they needed a more marketable symbol for the Montgomery Bus Boycott and the Civil Rights Movements. As mentioned, Rosa Parks was perfect for the symbolic mission of representing the ideal model of a dignified and older protestor against injustice—mature, light-colored, a self-made working woman, and already a respected member of the Civil Rights Movements.

Parks' qualifications to serve as a symbol of a national protest movement was the very antithesis of the fifteen-year-old Claudette, despite her own maturity and smarts.

In this sense, Claudette was even discriminated against by her own African American people, leaders of Montgomery's black community, and the top representatives of the Civil Rights Movement, because she was unfairly—still another kind of prejudice suffered by her—seen as a young troublemaker. In the end, she simply failed to meet the special requirements of a symbolic and marketable image like Parks, who then became known as the "Mother of the Civil Rights Movement."

Ironically, the relationship and situation of Claudette Colvin in relation to Rosa Parks can be seen in striking analogous ways in the John Ford 1962 film *The Man Who Shot Liberty Valance*. Ford's fascinating story is about a man who became a hero for having allegedly killed a notorious outlaw and town bully, who garnered a widespread popularity that lifted him into the lofty realm of territorial and then state politics in the Old West.

But in fact, the heroics of the film's hero were based on nothing more than an enduring romantic myth, because he never killed the famous outlaw Liberty Valance upon which his fame rested. Indeed, it was another man—obscure and forgotten—who had committed the heroic deed in eliminating the town's and area's great villain. Consequently, he never received recognition for ending the outlaw's life and died on obscurity. Indeed, in much the same way, so Claudette was forgotten for having been the first hero of the Civil Rights Movement, while Parks became a legend and icon as the first heroine of the protest movement and basked in the spotlight.

Therefore, in the supreme irony in the end, Claudette was not only rejected by her own people but also by the very people's movement that she had sparked in dramatic fashion by way of a remarkable exhibition of courage at great risk to herself when on her own—perhaps an appropriate, although tragic and sad ultimate fate in having been relegated to obscurity for decades, because she had sparked both the Montgomery Bus Boycott and the Civil Rights Movement on her own and by way of her own personal decisions based on black heroes and heroines (Harriet Tubman and Sojourner Truth were her foremost heroines), Biblical lessons, past racial injustices and horrors, and a moral and religious faith.

In this regard and compared to the adults who she knew only talked and complained about Jim Crow abuses, Claudette was certainly ahead of her time. Most of all, she knew that she was on the right side of history and that God was on her side in her darkest hour: the all-important dual inspirational moral influences that gave her great moral strength and courage to openly defy America's Apartheid system on her own.

All in all, this is the dramatic story of the remarkable young woman who started it all for the Civil Rights Movement and did what had never been done in Montgomery to shame the older generations of blacks, which was not her goal. For their entire lives, these older and long-oppressed second class citizens had accepted the humiliation of their lives for decades, as if it were a natural part of life, but not Claudette Colvin.

In striking contrast, Claudette was the very opposite in attitude and instinct to the people of the older generation. She instinctively knew that a new day and new time was sure to come at long last and one that was entirely overdue—the beginning of a true social revolution that would shake the Southern world to the core and lead to Jim Crow's death. In the end, therefore, this shy, reserved, and slight teenager, who wore thick-rimmed glasses and loved history with all her heart, was in fact the true mother of the Civil Rights Movement.

By doing what no one, black or white, thought that anyone would ever do and by dreaming the impossible dream, she inspired Rosa Parks and Martin Luther King to become more active on the protest front and straight into the pages of history. They spearheaded with the protest movement nine months later and after Claudette accomplished a host of groundbreaking milestones in the quest for equal rights and the winning of freedom for all—a true American heroine whose bravery and distinguished place in history in the struggle for human rights in America. Indeed, at only age fifteen, Claudette provided a most distinguished and meaningful profile in courage of a kind simply not at all found in the pages of Senator Kennedy's highly-acclaimed Pulitzer Prize winning book.

For ample good reason, Claudette astounded the black community, including NAACP leaders, by doing what others did not even dare to think about doing entirely on their own against the seemingly limitless power of white authority, both city and state, by striking a blow against legal segregation that was unconstitutional and immoral, as she knew to be the case in her heart and mind. From the depths of poverty and a broken home while mired in the poorest black section, King Hill, of Montgomery, she boldly embarked upon her own personal struggle not only for black rights, but also for human rights in general by deciding to fight back against the gross injustices that surrounded her like a curse.

At the time, perhaps a sympathetic white woman, Virginia Durr, a maverick and socialite of Montgomery, Alabama, who supported the great goal of desegregation, perhaps said it best: "I just can't explain how this little girl [age fifteen and slight in build] was so brave" and bold to follow her dictates of moral conscience, becoming the first Civil Rights Movements pioneer who initiated the most important black social and political movement of the twentieth century that changed America and the world.

Phillip Thomas Tucker, Ph.D.
Central Florida
April 23, 2020

Chapter I

Dark Days for African Americans

The year of 1955, only a decade after the end of the Second World War, was significant for America and especially for African Americans. Claudette Colvin turned fifteen on September 5, 1954, and her whole life was ahead of her. She was a typical black student, although more studious and serious minded, at Booker T. Washington High School in Montgomery, Alabama.

In her own words about a very common background and the most humble of beginnings like for most African Americans in the Deep South, "I was born Claudette Austin, September 5, 1939, in Birmingham, Alabama." Birmingham was located in the hill country, the southern edge of the Appalachian Mountains, around 90 miles northwest of the state capital of Montgomery.

Ironically, she had been named by her mother, Mary Ann Gadson who had married C. P. Austin, after movie star Claudette Colbert. The pretty infant girl, in Claudette's words, received the name Claudette because "we both had high cheekbones." Born in France in 1903, Colbert was a natural beauty with high cheekbones and dark, reddish hair. She emerged as a leading starlet during the age of classic Hollywood films.

It is not known, but Claudette's mother, Mary Ann Gadson who took the last name of Gadson because of her second marriage, might also have been inspired by Colbert's hit 1934 movie *Cleopatra*, because of its African connection that revealed a rich chapter of black history.

This epic film was directed by gifted Cecil B. DeMille, who was one of Hollywood's greatest directors. However, Claudette's mother most likely was inspired to bestow the name of Claudette on her new daughter by the 1939 film *Drums along the Mohawk*. In this popular film, Claudette Colbert played the lead female role of a strong and attractive pioneer woman named Lana Borst, who had settled with her husband along the remote New York's frontier during the American Revolution.

After all, Mary Ann was pregnant of the time with Claudette at this time in 1939, and she might have seen the film in one of Birmingham's segregated theaters. Symbolically, Claudette's love of history was perhaps appropriate given the fact that Claudette Colbert, who was voted the 12th greatest actress in the age of classic Hollywood films, when she starred in a good many popular historical films during the 1930s.

Although she had been born in Alabama's largest city of Birmingham, Claudette would evolve very much into a country girl. Partly because of economic reasons and with her mother's marriage having fallen apart in Birmingham, fate intervened to change Claudette's life in dramatic fashion.

In Claudette's words: "When I was just a baby, I went off to live with my great-aunt, Mary Ann Colvin, and my great-uncle, Q. P. Colvin, in a little country town called Pine Level," Alabama. Surrounded by the dense pine forests from which its name was derived, Pine Level was located on the main road between Birmingham, around 80 miles to the northwest, and Montgomery, which was situated about 30 miles to the southeast.

Here, in amid the rural environment of Montgomery County, Pine Level was an old community of friendly people, black and white of the lower class. The first post office of quiet and rural Pine Level was established in 1839. This isolated community in central Alabama was also known as Pine Tucky. In one of the ironies of history, young Rosa Parks, then known as Rosa Louise McCauley, lived in Pine Level as a child more than a generation before Claudette.

This formative period at Pine Level was one of the best times in Claudette's life during the 1940s. As she fondly remembered: "Mary Ann and Q. P. are the ones I call Mom and Dad. They were a lot older than my birth parents [and] I loved then both, and I was happy to be with them." She also called "Dad" by the name of "Daddy P.Q" in their close family unit.

Even more, Claudette loved country life in a tiny community of poor blacks, and fondly remembered Pine Level well into her adult life. Here, African Americans either farmed small plots of poor land to scratch out a living among the pine thickets or worked for poor whites as sharecroppers in the fields of small farmers—a typical rural community of the Deep South.

For Claudette, who was thin and tall for her age—ideal physical qualities for a tomboy, this was a time of innocence and fun because she basked in seemingly every aspect of rural life.

Everyone was poor, but self-sufficient and possessed a simple dignify because their lives were tied closely to the land and they were a God-fearing people who constantly read the pages of the Holy Bible.

Even more, a good deal of love abounded in a contented life, which was made happier when little sister Delphine joined them in the little country house of "Mom and Dad." In her own words: "I grew up [in Pine Level] in a quartet—Mary Ann, Q. P., Delphine, and me. And our dog, Bell, and two horses and lots of chickens, cows, and pigs."

To young Claudette who was the very definition of a tomboy who loved to run through the fields of tall grass and climb trees when she was known by the nickname of "Coot," Pine Level was heaven on earth to her. She enjoyed the wide open spaces of the countryside and rural life in general.

As she explained of this happy time in her life: "Pine Level didn't have much more than a few shacks for the share-cropper families [who worked for white farmers], a schoolhouse, a church, and a general store, but I was at home in all of it. I floated free, and slept in the homes of my mom's friends as much as my own bed. They all raised me together."

In addition, Claudette also began to develop a keen interest in history from what she learned from local residents of Pine Level, which had survived the Civil War and Yankee invasion. Here, in Pine Level, she learned about local Civil War history which was rich, hearing stories from those blacks who lived in the small community northwest of the state capital of Montgomery.

It is not known but the distinct possibility existed that ancestors of some of Pine Level's black residents had fought the Rebels in USCT, United States Colored Troops, regiments (infantry, cavalry and artillery) during the Civil War.

Therefore, with her new-found sense of history gained from the environment of Pine Level, Claudette recalled how when staying at the comfortable house of "mom's best friend" which was the largest in town, "Annie and I used to look out the attic window and pretend the Yankee soldiers were about ready to come charging over the hill."

Significantly, these early years in Pine Level were all-important in molding and shaping Claudette's character.

The formative period bestowed her with a strong work ethic, that transferred into a love of study and school, a free spirit, and independent nature from the rural experience and country living—qualities that were much different from many city blacks, who had never grown-up in a rural environment.

In her own words that revealed her quest and thirst for knowledge, "I loved school."

Moving to Montgomery

Then, Claudette's life again took a sudden and abrupt turn when she turned eight in 1957. At that time, Mary Ann Colvin inherited a modest house in Montgomery, and they left Pine Level to start anew in the city. While growing up in Montgomery, Claudette's insular world in the poorest back section of town, known as King Hill, was the complete opposite of the white America, especially the rapidly-expanding middle class in the suburbs. Here, in northeast Montgomery and far from her beloved Pine Level, Claudette was destined to come of age, when the curse of Jim Crow ruled the land with an iron fist.

The common misconception that these were carefree years of the "Baby Boom" generation—the vast majority of whites enjoyed a comfortable middle class status because of the postwar boom—during the 1950s was certainly not the case for African Americans. Ironically, this dismal Jim Crow situation even applied to those brave black veterans, such as the Tuskegee Airmen who fought for their country in the skies over Europe, including Germany, and won fame during the Second World War.

Like in all of America's wars going all the way back to the French and Indian War (known on the Seven Years' War in Europe and the first world war) that ended in 1763 when England conquered Canada and including in the

Civil War, black fighting men made contributions in the war effort. Indeed, more than 200,000 black troops served in uniforms of blue and faithfully served their country from 1863 to 1865. However, regardless of which war, including the American Revolution, blacks had been always unable to fully enjoy the fruits of victory as equal citizens with full rights, after these conflicts were won.

After Reconstruction during the post-Civil War period, locally-elected politicians of the Southern states, including Alabama, systematically stripped African Americans of their rights as full United States citizens that they had won in the Civil War and had been guaranteed in the United States Constitution.

Tragically, such was also the case of African Americans and black veterans who had fought their country's battles after the end of the Second World War, especially in the South during an unprecedented period of domestic prosperity—the President Dwight David "Ike" Eisenhower's years of peace and plenty in a robust postwar economy, after the former GI's once again joined the work force.

In 1955 when Claudette Colvin made her fateful decision to defy white authority and segregationist Jim Crow laws by refusing to leave her bus seat and go to the back of the bus for a white passenger, Disneyland opened in Anaheim, California, and the television series "Gunsmoke," which was destined to become the most popular western in history, appeared on CBS during America's age of innocence.

But as noted, this tranquil and happy period was simply not the case for African Americans. They were oppressed as second class citizens, especially in the Deep South, in America's own Apartheid system, which was deeply-entrenched and enshrined in custom and law by the states.

After all of the many sacrifices that Americans made in the total war effort for four years during the Second World War, these were the good times of the 1950s for the vast majority of whites, but not for the majority of blacks, especially in the Deep South. American fighting men had destroyed fascism and liberated Europe, but blacks had not been liberated in the United States in the ultimate tragic irony.

Indeed, in what was a national disgrace and tragedy that even the enemy, including Adolf Hitler's Nazi Germany, had employed in its own anti-American propaganda, African Americans, young and old, had yet to be truly liberated from the nightmare of institutionalized racism in the South, because of discriminatory Jim Crow racial laws that had existed for more the better part of a century.

For most Americans and as mentioned, the 1950s was the boom period and the happy "I Like Ike" (President Dwight David Eisenhower) years that white historians have long described as the most innocent eras in American history. Partly the result of the prolific writings of "Baby Boom" authors, screenwriters, and historians well into the twenty-first century, this distinctive period has been thoroughly romanticized and idealized, including to this day.

In fact, this distinctive period in American life has been most commonly portrayed as the most feel good period in American history in which society's seemingly endless virtues shined brightly, as if America possessed no internal social problems or contradictions, especially when it came to race.

At this time in 1955 when Claudette made her bold decision to stand firm in her defiant act of conscience despite orders from the white bus driver and white police officers to vacate her seat on fateful March 2, most Baby Boomers were still under the age of 10 at this time.

During this period of tranquility, white families were headed primarily by former servicemen who had served their country during the Second World War and the Korean conflict. Here, they raised their families in the white suburbs that spanned for considerable distances beyond America's major cities—an idyllic setting that was unique because of relatively little violence, domestic trouble, or crime compared to the inner cities.

But, of course, this common stereotype of best of all times for America in the 1950s was partly a popular myth, because black America faced a harsh environment that cruelly mocked the core egalitarian concepts of the American dream and the United States Constitution, as if they were meant only for whites.

As noted, the black world, especially in the Deep South and in the impoverished inner cities of the North, was the opposite of life in the white suburbs of America's major cities, this pristine white world of the "Baby Boomers" in America's sprawling suburbs. In fact, life in the white suburbs was the very antithesis of black America across the breath of the South and also in many parts of the North.

The segregated black world was a living nightmare for America's blacks in the Deep South, especially in Montgomery, where African Americans were severely oppressed by laws, customs, and society like no other people in America only because of their color. To generations of African Americans, daily life completely mocked the bold words and lofty promising of equality as enshrined in the United States Constitution and the Declaration of Independence.

Even more, the South's dehumanizing Jim Crow laws were perfectly tailored to keep an entire people entrapped in poverty and isolated segregated communities as lowly second class citizens in almost every Southern city in the land. America's system of legalized oppression and discrimination was so insidiously effective in creating a permanently oppressed underclass in the so-called "land of the free" that it had provided the perfect model for the heartlessness of the most sinister government in the history of the twentieth century, Nazi Germany.

Indeed, Nazi German leaders, lawyers, and legislators looked around the world for a model to oppress the Jewish people in the 1930s. The Nazi's found a perfect model in the Jim Crow laws of the Deep South, and basically applied it to Germany.

In the greatest irony of America and the so-called "greatest generation" of Americans who helped to win the Second World War, blacks across the South were treated much like the Jewish people in Germany during the 1930s, long before the war's outbreak. This was America's ugliest racial and social reality because more than 125,00 black servicemen had served overseas in the United States Army, Merchant Marine, and the Navy during the Second World War: a tragic situation that brought great shame upon the United States.

While black fighting men lost their lives in the European theater in battling for their country against the march of fascism, the black families, including mothers, sisters, and daughters, in the South continued to suffer as oppressed second class citizens under the oppression of Jim Crow discrimination, which was essentially a form of fascism as seen in Nazi Germany.

During the 1940s, the ultimate irony was that black civilians and soldiers were extremely patriotic and loved their country just like whites. The African Americans of Pine Level amid the rural countryside were no different. For instance, when Claudette was being raised on a small, self-sufficient farm at Pine Level, the Colvin extended family hated Hitler and fascism like white Americans. In the tradition of a humor-based African American culture, black folk, who knew that Hitler's regime was based on the concept of white superiority, possessed their own unique manifestations of patriotism that were mixed with a sense of humor in this rural setting, which was located northwest of Montgomery.

In the words of Claudette Colvin, "while WWII was going on [in 1945 when she was only age 6], whenever one of our hens [in the chicken coop on the farm] would lay a bad egg we'd mark it with an 'H' –for Hitler." This revealing statement by Claudette has provided an interesting example of the sense of patriotism that existed in the small black community even in a rural area. After all, a number of blacks from his rural area outside Montgomery and on the road to Birmingham were serving their country in the European theater during the war years, fighting and dying for their homeland and the people.

As subsequent events demonstrated, it was most symbolic that Claudette had been born on Sunday September 3, 1939, which was no ordinary day in the annals of world history. This fateful day was a turning point in world history because it ensured that America was fated to embark upon a people's crusade to defeat the relentless march of fascism and Nazi Germany, just as Wednesday March 2, 1955, when Claudette was destined to spark a people's movement that also helped to defeat America's own fascist-like system of Jim Crow and changed the world. In many ways and a fact often overlooked by historians, Claudette's life seemed to have significant historical overtones and influences from the beginning.

On this third day of September 1939, Great Britain and France officially declared war on Nazi Germany to begin a "supreme cataclysm" in Winston Churchill's words, because of its overpowering invasion—the blitzkrieg—of Poland on September 1. Therefore, the day that Claudette was born was the official beginning of the Second World War, and in 1955—ten years after the war's end—she initiated the people's movement for equal rights that played a key role in vanquishing America's own special and deeply-entrenched domestic form of fascism that was Jim Crow.

As noted, Nazi German's legal discrimination and oppression of the Jewish people during the 1930s was largely modeled on America's Jim Crow system. Because Jim Crow had so effectively discriminated against African Americans, it was then applied by Nazi Germany to the Jewish people to keep them completely separated from the German people for primarily the same reasons—to strip them of economic and political power and human rights, especially to ensure that there was no social intermixing.

Sharing a perverse heritage, both white Southerners and Nazi's were obsessed with the misguided concept of racial purity and the core tenets of white superiority. In part, this distorted policy eventually led Nazi Germany to its doom.

In truth and as noted, what Claudette and other blacks under Jim Crow oppressive faced in Montgomery was essentially a domestic form of fascism, which America had fought against during the Second World War and at a time around 1945 when she and his sister had mocked Hitler. When hens laid bad eggs at Pine Level farm, Claudette attached the name Hitler to them.

Although fascism, which had also thrived in Italy and Japan to combine with an aggressive imperialism, was defeated at great cost in lives and resources when Berlin, Germany, finally fell to Russian Armies in April 1945, this cancerous and insidious form of oppression, as experienced by the Jewish people in Germany during the 1930s, was alive and well in Jim Crow discrimination across the South.

This then was the real and most forgotten enemy of Claudette Colvin during the struggle for equal rights, as black people fully realized while living under an American Apartheid system, which was comparable to the Nazi's Apartheid system directed against the Jewish people.

Indeed, after Hitler came to power in 1934, top Nazi statesmen, judges, and lawyers—the best and brightest in Germany's legal system—searched for a perfect model of oppression to subjugate the Jewish people, who were a prosperous and highly-educated class, to force them into a permanent second class status with legal discrimination enshrined in the law. For the creation of a new race regime based on the concept of white German superiority and alleged Jewish inferiority to justify a legal oppression, they found an ideal model in the Jim Crow laws of racist legislation in the Deep South.

As early as the 1920s, Hitler and other Nazi leaders had praised America's racist system of oppression that had been made legal and the law of the land across the Deep South to create a permanent underclass of black people in the so-called "home of the brave and land of the free." Hitler had even complimented America and the overall effectiveness of its harsh race laws in the pages of *Mein Kampf*.

America, especially the Deep South, provided the model for racial legislation that legalized racial discrimination that led to the infamous Nuremberg Laws. This was an insidious development because these discriminatory laws officially created second class citizens of the Jewish people that ultimately led to the horrors of the Holocaust.

Quite simply, Hitler and other Nazi leaders were inspired by the awful truth of America's legal mistreatment and abuse of African Americans, which was the law of the land—the kind of unjust laws that Claudette and other black freedom fighters battled against in the name of the right and freedom for all.

The harsh racial world of Claudette Colvin was truly a personal nightmare for African Americans.

Germany's anti-Jewish discrimination laws of the 1930s and the Jim Crow laws of the Deep South of the 1950s, especially legal segregation, were "mirror images" of each other.

But, ironically, while the discriminatory Nuremberg Laws, that unleashed mobs of right-wing Germans, especially the Brown Shirts, on the Jewish people to plunder and kill Hebrews in the 1930s, the comparable discriminatory system of a fascist-like system of oppression, based on the concept of white supremacy, allowed whites to plunder and kill blacks, especially by mob lynching, in the Deep South. These seemingly endless tragedies occurred during the course of Claudette's teenage years to infuriate her to no end.

Ironically, to their credit, some Nazi lawyers and legislatures, although accepting of America's concept of white supremacy and applying it to Germany during the 1930s, rejected some of America's Jim Crow laws as too harsh and too racist for Germany.

But in the end and as noted, the racial laws of Jim Crow were basically transferred to Nazi Germany to the everlasting shame of America.

A Powerful Religious Faith

In Claudette Colvin's words of despair about her harsh world of racial segregation that she began to more deeply contemplate with greater horror as she became older, because the racial injustices were all around her and seemed to have no end: "The biggest mystery of all was how the white man came to dominate us. In the South, it was taught that white people were better than blacks. Somehow, they were the masters and we were there to work for them. My mom said white people thought God made them special. My Sunday school teacher said we had been cursed by one of Noah's sons. I didn't buy that at all. To me, God loved everyone. Why would He curse just us? My mom thought she was as good as anyone else. So did I. One day I told my pastor, Reverend H. H. Johnson, 'I don't want to serve a God that would have a cursed race'."

In the tranquil country environment of Pine Level before the family moved to Montgomery 1957 and as noted, Claudette experienced her most formative period that forged the depth of her character. During this formative period, she was completely in tune to both nature and God because they were one in the same, when Claudette was living in Pine Level. As Claudette marveled at the pristine and tranquil world of nature around her and the easy pace of rural life, she became more devout, because God's handiwork in nature was all around her.

Consequently, Claudette described how her Christian faith also reached a high point at this time: "I was very religious. Annie and I played church together out behind her house, setting up chairs and doing services . . . The second Sunday of every month the Reverend H. H. Johnson came out from Montgomery and pastored a service at our little church in the country."

After moving southeast to Montgomery when age eight, Claudette's close experiences with nature and God and their symbiotic relationship that had been forged at Pine Level never left her. She and her family lived in Montgomery's poorest black neighborhood, which was known simply as King Hill. Here, in the northeast part of Montgomery and located on a small hilltop in the black community nestled between two larger white neighborhoods, the family lived in a small frame house.

King Hill's poverty was evident by unpaved the street, no streetlights, and only outhouses in the rear of residences, almost like a rural community far from Montgomery—much like a larger Pine Level amid an urban setting in part because the people were close-knot. Claudette knew all about the poverty on King Hill, which consisted of "just three streets on top of a hill on the edge of town."

But like at Pine Level that was located northwest of Montgomery and just northeast of the city's Alabama State College, the good people of the King Hill community helped each other to get through the daily challenges and struggles of life in the manner of a large kinship group.

Here, Claudette found a safe and secure home around a good many friendly neighbors at King Hill, and, of course, a loving family. Like at Pine Level, neighbors looked out for each other. Although she still regretted having had to leave behind country life behind in a small black community amid the rural countryside, Claudette was now part of the urban environment of the state capital, Montgomery.

Hutchinson Street Baptist Church, Claudette's main house of worship, and the King Hill Church of Christ, to a lesser extent, lifted Claudette's spiritual life to new heights, especially on Sunday, and that of other people of

King Hill to a level unimaginable to less religious whites of the state capital of Montgomery.

Living in a city, which was part of Montgomery County, that was completely dominated by the ugly realities of Jim Crow, she was early angered upon visiting downtown Montgomery. In Claudette's own words: "We could shop in white stores—they'd take our money all right—but they wouldn't let us try anything on. I never went into a fitting room like white people did [and] When Delphine [her younger sister] and I needed shoes, my mom would trace the shape of our feet on a brown paper bag and we'd carry the outline to the store because we weren't allowed to try the shoes on."

But a greater shock awaited Claudette, because the world of Jim Crow in Montgomery became an even greater part of a daily routine as she was older. Frustrating, degrading, and humiliating experiences in the oppressive lives of blacks, from children to grandparents, in Montgomery became only too common. Sadly, the ugliness of all manner of racial discrimination was basically accepted as just part of life by African Americans, and a tragic aspect of Montgomery that could not be changed.

Another turning point came in Claudette's Colvin's life came after she entered high school at Booker T. Washington, when a central tragedy struck that deeply affected her life. A close friend and fellow Booker T. Washington student from her neighborhood of King Hill was framed for allegedly having raped a white woman, Jeremiah Reeves, age sixteen.

Then, other similar confessions were forced from Jeremiah in the mysterious darkness of the police station, which was manned by all white officers. These were all trumped-up charges and phony confessions, which had been forced from him by threats from police officers. The charges piled up with the goal of seating him in the electric chair, and they were destined to stick.

Born in Montgomery in 1935, Jeremiah was a gregarious and carefree spirit who was a popular senior. Handsome, a stylish dresser, and a skilled Jazz drummer in the school band, Jeremiah was a special person, who was beloved by his fellow students. Positive, likeable, and optimistic about life, he was also a sentimental poetic who wrote lengthy poems from his jail cell. Jeremiah never lost the hope that he would eventually be set free—a vain hope in the end.

But as noted, there was no hope at all for the young man. Jeremiah's fate had already been sealed when he was forced to confess to multiple charges of rape by overzealous and racist white police officers. They had saddled him with allegedly breaking in other homes and raping six other white women—phony charges that the white jury believed or assumed were legitimate to send him to the electric chair.

In a travesty of justice and to Claudette Colvin's horror, Jeremiah was executed at age twenty-two in

Montgomery by the State of Alabama on March 28, 1958, when he reached adulthood and was no longer a juvenile.

In the gross injustice of Reeves' arrest on false charges struck the students like a thunderbolt, especially Claudette, infuriating the students of Booker T. Washington High School. Besides causing her to lose some more of her innocence, the tragic case of Jeremiah Reeves additionally radicalized Claudette and other teens. She had faithfully written letters to Jeremiah in jail, joined in rallies that supported him, and collected money to pay his lawyers, but it was all to no avail.

To the very end, Reeves always maintained his innocence. But in this Jim Crow regime and as mentioned, he had forced to confess to whatever the white officers said because they had applied heavy pressure, including the threat of immediate death in the electric chair. Dr. Martin Luther King spoke out against "the sin committed against Jeremiah Reeves," and viewed him as a sainted martyr like the people of Montgomery's black community.

Indeed, Reeves became a martyr who had been still another tragic victim of the entire Jim Crow system and an omnipresent racism, and he was never forgotten by Claudette. Jeremiah continued to live in the heart and mind of Claudette Colvin, as long as she lived.

Claudette was changed forever by the horrors of Jim Crow when radicalized by the never-ending abuse and racial injustice more than ever before. She concluded how "Jeremiah Reeve's arrest was the turning point in my life [and] I was furious when I found out what had happened.

Jeremiah lived right below us on the Hill . . . There were rumors that the jailers . . . tortured him [and] The hypocrisy of it made me so angry! Black girls were extremely vulnerable [to lecherous white men and] now they were going hold Jeremiah for years as a minor just so they could legally execute him when he came of age. That changed me. That put anger in me [and] I stayed angry about Jeremiah Reeves for a long time."

During the Reeves tragedy and while he waited in prison for years on death row to be executed as an adult which was a long-running torment for the young man all in itself, Claudette continued to feel a deep sense of outrage at the gross injustices that she saw every day and all around her. As if hoping to forget the racial horror that surrounded her and had cursed black people for so long and reasons that she never could fully understood because they made so little sense, Claudette buried herself in her studies at Booker T. Washington High School. But Claudette Colvin could never forget what had happened to her friend Jeremiah, and she would never be the same.

However, everything now had new meaning for Claudette, because she looked at the world much differently than before. Quite simply and as noted, Claudette had lost much of her youthful innocence at a young age since having moved with her family from the country to the city, where harsh racial realities dominated all aspects of black lives. For reasons that continued to increase, she now listened to her favorite teacher,

Geraldine Nesbit, more intently than before about the lessons of black history and with a much keener interest.

When the students of Claudette's class at Booker T. Booker, where handsome Jeremiah Reeves had once walked the halls with pride, a winning smile, and high hopes for a bright future, studied the American Revolution, "we discussed Patrick Henry's speech—'Give me liberty or give me death"—and applied it to our own situation."

Indeed, most of all what was needed in Montgomery was an organized black revolution to overturn the seemingly endless racial injustices of America's Apartheid system and the legal entrenchment of Jim Crow that had made black lives, including young Claudette Colvin, miserable for so long.

In this harsh, unforgiving racial environment of the big city compared to serene and quaint Pine Level, Claudette learned her lessons well, understanding how the past still applied to the present day. In her own words: "Miss Nesbit made us see that we had a history, too—that our story didn't begin by being captured and chained and thrown onto a boat. There had been life and culture before that [and] I grew in confidence."

Even more and although still a shy, young lady who was serious-minded and loved school with all her heart, especially black history, Claudette steadily grew in spirit, confidence, and content of character over time. She began to better understand the nuances of not only black history, but also more about racism in general.

As she described how her favorite history teacher who also served as an inspirational model, Miss Josie Lawrence "was the blackest teacher in the whole school [and] She'd say, 'I'm a real African. I'm a pure-blooded African" [and] She was proud of it [and] She taught us all the different nations of Africa and the periods of African history. It all made sense to me. I wasn't ashamed of my thick lips and broad nose and coarse hair."

Like no other student at Booker T. Washington High School, Claudette was a devout lover of black history and culture, which bolstered her self-esteem and self-image, which had been severely battered by having to live for years under racism. Even more and all the while, she was maturing and evolving into a black nationalist, who loved her people, culture, and history, which were factors that became a source of intense pride.

For such reasons and with sage insight and a wise maturity beyond her fifteen years of age, a determined Claudette began to form her own personal vision of her own place in the most racist of worlds based on all of her collective wisdom and accumulated rage at seemingly countless racial injustices.

In no certain terms and with a single-minded sense of determination that could not be shaken, she came to a bold conclusion about her future that guaranteed that neither she or her life would never be the same: "I began to form a mission for myself. I was going [to] be like Harriet Tubman and go North to liberate my people. I admired Harriet Tubman more than anyone else I read about—her courage, the pistol she wore, the fact that she never lost a passenger on the Underground Railroad. I wasn't going to Alabama State [College in Montgomery], where they taught you how to teach school but didn't teach you how to get your freedom."

Claudette Colvin was rapidly evolving well beyond her less serious-minded peers in terms of moral conscience, which combined with a feisty personal attitude of defiance and an increasingly proactive stance that was implanted in her mind: a committed and whole-hearted believer in the necessity of spirited resistance to racial oppression and injustice in the tradition of her hero, Harriet Tubman.

Chapter II

The Value of Black History Month 1955 and the Forgotten Young Woman That Gave Birth to the Civil Rights Movement

A precious gift that proved invaluable and absolutely priceless to the shaping of a young lady's character and sense of determination was bestowed to the students of the junior class at Booker T. Washington High School, Montgomery, Alabama, in February 1955.

At this time, the arrival of the warmth of an Alabama spring brought a feeling that something new was in the air. But, at this time, neither the increase in heat or humidity, that told of winter's end and promised nice days ahead, had become unbearable like in July and August.

Outside the high school grounds in the southwestern part of town located amid rolling terrain of high ground—hence the name of King Hill for Claudette's neighborhood—and bluffs that overlooked the wide, brown waters of the Alabama River, the magnolia trees and the dogwoods were sprouting white flowers, while the crape myrtles were covered in red flowers in the spring-like weather. Montgomery was especially picturesque at this time of year, when all of nature was once again coming alive with the bright sunshine and warmer temperatures. The heat and humidity seemed to get getting higher with each new day in late February and early March. But the overall freshness and beauty of early March in central Alabama and enjoyed by Claudette and her fellow students was marred by the harsh racial realities that completely dominated Montgomery.

Indeed, perhaps no major city in all of the Deep South was more stereotypical in its strict adherence to old Southern traditions and ugly racial legacies, especially its Jim Crow laws and entrenched inequitable way of life, in every way than Alabama's capital, Montgomery.

For instance and most appropriately, the Alabama River port town of Montgomery, founded in 1819 like the state itself that was no longer a territory, became the first capital of the newly-established Confederacy in February 1861. At that time, slave-owner President Jefferson Davis, who lived in the White House of the Confederacy that was located on Washington Street, presided over the birth of a new Southern nation based on the institution of slavery—the newest republic and a true experiment in nationhood.

In fact and unfortunately for its black citizens, including young Claudette Colvin, Montgomery was even more traditionally Southern in the harsh extremity of its racism and intolerance than most Southern cities, even those located elsewhere in the heart of the Deep South. Tragically for blacks in Montgomery, including Claudette, the state capital was very much the epitome of the horrors of the unforgiving Jim Crow world of legalized discrimination and prejudice that was the law of the land. These harsh racial laws, both city and state, were based on the most extreme and grossest of injustices and inequality.

Unfortunately for Claudette Colvin, how did Montgomery become perhaps America's most heartless and racist city for its black citizens by the 1950s with its permanent entrenchment of Jim Crow? In the histories of the Civil Rights Movement, this question has been seldom, if ever, asked or explored in depth, but the contours of an extremely violent past partly explained the present at that time. But to understand how and why the horrors of Jim Crow developed in Alabama in the first place, a look at events in Alabama's past is required and beyond even the factor of slavery.

Long before the outbreak of the Civil War on April 12, 1861 when Confederate cannon opened fire on Fort Sumter in the harbor of Charleston, South Carolina, Alabama possessed an especially harsh racial history. This storied past that white Alabamians relished included chapters of brutal warfare, massacre, and genocide long before the arrival of large numbers of African Americans to work Alabama's fertile land of cotton, which produced the "White Gold" to enrich the planter class.

The Creek War of 1813-1813 resulted in the systematic destruction of the war faction, the so-called Red Sticks who sought to protect their culture and lands from relentless white encroachment, of the Creek Nation. Invading United States troops and volunteer militia units from Tennessee, Georgia, and Mississippi laid waste to the native homeland of the Creek people.

To the shock of many men, especially officers, in the ranks, one-sided American victories deep in Creek country, which was a fertile, virgin land, were won by hard-hitting tactics that included slaughter and massacre. Even many Creek women and children were killed without mercy by the white interlopers. In the end, the Creeks never had a chance because the invaders of the Creek homeland across today's Alabama possessed the technical edge in weapons, especially cannon.

Consequently, the ill-armed, disorganized Red Sticks, who fought as individuals because of their traditional concept of ancient hit-and-run and ambush warfare, never had a change against the superior firepower of the white invaders and their hardest hitting general, Andrew Jackson.

The thorough defeat of the Creeks and the winning of Alabama for massive white settlement resulted in the establishment of the Alabama territory with the securing of 21 million acres of Creek lands. This vast expanse of lands was opened up to large-scale cotton culture and slavery to create a prosperous land of cotton. Quite simply, the Creek War had resulted in not only genocide of Native American people, but also ethnic cleansings on a massive scale not previously seen in the annals of American history: a gross byproduct of the metaphysics of Indian hating that had existed in America since the colonial period.

Therefore, because of Alabama having perhaps the darkest and most grim racial history of any state in the Deep South, including in regard to the lynching of blacks by white mobs, it was all-important in the fertile minds of the dedicated black teachers at Booker T. Washington High School that they should place a heavy and special emphasis on black history. They were determined to bolster the pride in themselves and their people of African heritage to improve the battered egos of young black people, like Claudette Colvin, in their formative years, because they had known only too well the unjust strictness of Jim Crow all their lives.

Consequently, as Claudette explained, "in 1955, my junior year, Miss Nesbitt and Miss Lawrence team-taught Negro History Week [or month in February]. We really got into it. We spent that whole February talking about the injustices we black people suffered every day in Montgomery—it was total immersion."

Rather than the near springtime beauty of the blooming flowers on the tall hardwood trees atop Montgomery's bluffs that overlooked the picturesque Alabama River, the real beauty that could be found at the high school, built of dark brick in the most plain style, for black students was the rich chapters of black history of a long-oppressed people that gifted black teachers, mostly dedicated women, presented to their students of this segregated school in southeast Montgomery.

The African American teachers at Booker T. Washington High School devoted the entire month of

February to the teaching of black history to young men and women, who badly-needed an enhanced dose of black pride for themselves, their culture and people, because of the dark legacies of Alabama history and Jim Crow. Clearly, these young minds that had been wrapped by the insidiousness of Jim Crow to the extent of them, especially black females, undertaking efforts of attempting to look as white as possible, desperately needed to know all about black heroes and heroines of a storied past.

Such an intensified, or crash course in this case, about the most stirring aspects of black history was most appropriate for Montgomery's black high school students. After all, Alabama had been a leading slave state, where cotton had been "king," during the decades of the antebellum period and large numbers of slaves had labored for generations in Alabama's fields of misery to leave an enduring dark legacy of an oppressed people.

But the hard-working black teachers of Booker T. Washington High School were not teaching about the accompanying horrors of cotton culture and the suffering of slaves that were too depressing to convey to young people in February 1955, because they were focused primarily on the most positive and uplifting examples that could be found in African American history. After all, these students were the descendants of the former slaves, who had mostly toiled in the sweltering cotton fields of Alabama during the antebellum and Civil War period.

Consequently, the subject of slavery was certainly nothing new or novel to these black students, because they had already heard more than enough stories about slavery's horrors from great grandparents and grandparents as part of the rich oral tradition of the African American people, while growing up in the heart of Dixie.

However, paradoxically, these young students could also personally relate to the searing subject of slavery, because they often almost felt that they themselves were caught in their own slavery-like environment of Jim Crow in Montgomery.

For all of these reasons throughout the weeks of February 1955, the young black students of Booker T. Washington High School literally soaked up their teachers' uplifting and inspirational words about the famous men and women of African descent from the pages of an incredibly rich history.

One excellent and neatly-dressed young student in particular in the history class during her junior year was especially attentive and fascinated by the heroic tales of black achievement and the dramatic lives of brave men and women, who had long struggled against the odds.

Tall and slim and blessed with traditional African features that gave no hint of any white blood, fifteen-year-old Claudette Colvin was the star of her junior class. She was a most serious student who appropriately wore black-rimmed reading glasses and naturally bookish in part because of her shyness. Claudette was quiet, serious-minded and studious unlike so many other students of her age. However, she possessed strong passions, undetected by others who did not know her well, that stirred deep inside her.

Claudette especially loved her talented teachers, who always went the extra mile when it came to the noble profession of teaching, especially black history. Consequently, this humble King Hill resident basked in what her teachers taught her during Black History Month throughout the still chilly February, before the arrival of spring.

Most of all, Claudette was in inquisitive and bright. She delighted in making mostly A's in her classes, but Claudette never mentioned or bragged about her smarts or successes to either family or her fellow students.

In keeping with her strong religious faith, she remained humble, modest,—as the Holy Bible emphasized for model Christian behavior—and extremely religious-minded, knowing that boasting and love of self were against God's will.

No doubt sitting in the front of the class since she was a straight A student who was a member of the Honor Society at Booker T. Washington, when the exciting chapters of black history was emphasized by her teachers throughout February 1955, Claudette excelled in her studies. She looked more studious than her peers because of her reading glasses: an appropriate scholarly appearance that was a perfect fit for Claudette's serious-mindedness, scholarly-bent, and maturity beyond her years.

For a high school junior of her age, Claudette possessed an old soul in many ways. As noted, she was quite dark in color and without any hint of white blood or traditional Caucasian features.

Like most students of her high school in southeast Montgomery, Claudette possessed the looks of her ancestors, who most likely hailed from West Africa, where they had been stolen and transported across the deadly "Middle Passage" to the New World in the nineteenth century.

In part because of this fact and her intense interest in Africans and black history, she personally related in the most intimate way to the exciting stories of black heroes and heroines, as taught by her favorite teacher, who was also one of the most dedicated instructors at Booker T. Washington High School, Geraldine Nesbitt. She was a graduate of Alabama State College in Montgomery, which Claudette desired to attend one day.

Throughout the month of February both at school and at home, Claudette especially thought deeply about two history lessons in particular because they were so inspiring to the depths of her soul and more than any other historical subjects: the remarkable stories of two of the most dynamic women of both the antebellum period and the Civil War: Maryland-born Harriett Tubman, who escaped slavery in 1849, and New York-born Sojourner Truth, who escape slavery in 1826.

Both of these women of courage and former slaves dedicated their lives to not only fighting against slavery, but also for the rights of women and for all oppressed people in general. Even more, Tubman and Sojourners also fought for women's rights for decades.

In part, Claudette closely and personally related to these two remarkable women because of the courage that they had long demonstrated against impossible odds and in fighting for the right. Even more, Tubman and Truth, who had been sold four times and more the Harriet, had proved that they had been on the right side of history in a day when women were considered decidedly inferior and incapable of achieving nothing more than cooking dinner, raising children, and engaging in other domestic roles.

Shattering the long-existing negative stereotypes about gender and race, Tubman helped to plan and lead one of the most daring Union raids of the Civil War deep in South Carolina in the midpoint of the Civil War: the audacious Combahee River raid, which included black soldiers who had been mostly former slaves like Tubman, of early June 1863.

With Tubman in the lead vessel with co-commander Colonel James Montgomery who had been a Kansas Jayhawker, this bold raid slashed into Confederate territory in a liberating mission that freed hundreds of slaves just west of the Sea Islands and South Carolina's Atlantic coast.

Additionally, Tubman and Truth were both very dark in color like Claudette, which also was a source of racial pride for her.

But most of all, she admired the daring and audacity of Tubman when she escaped from slavery and then took the great risk of repeatedly returning to the Eastern Shore of Maryland to rescue other slaves, including her own parents and siblings. Tubman became a leading conductor of the Underground Railroad throughout the 1850s, while compiling a stirring record of heroics over a period of decades.

Although life was severe and tough for blacks in Montgomery because of the discrimination of the Jim Crow laws that corrupted every aspect of black daily life and fueled Claudette's anger from having been victimized for her entire life by an entrenched discriminatory system at no fault of her own, Claudette understood that her own personal struggle against Jim Crow paled in comparison to that of Tubman and Truth.

Naturally, this comparison to past black heroines and racial situations provided the only way that allowed her to remain positive and upbeat in the depths of an oppressive system, while allowing Claudette to feel better about her negative situation that seemed less repressive.

But the greatest lesson from history that was imparted to Claudette was that the power of religion and faith eventually triumphed over the most insidious evil.

After all, both Harriet Tubman and Sojourner Truth were devout women, who had placed their faith completely in God and his wisdom for divine protection.

With her trademark sage wisdom, Truth had emphasized how, "religion without humanity is very poor human stuff."

And Tubman, known as the "Black Moses," knew that her successes were only because, "Oh Lord! You've been wid me in [all my] troubles."

The factor of religion was yet another reason that explained why Claudette closely identified with these two amazing women because they were so religiously-inspired and followed the Holy Bible's moral lessons and commandments just like this serious-minded teenager, who called King Hill home.

Outsized Dreams

Most of all, Claudette learned about life from studying the ups and down of Harriet Tubman during the tortuous course of her life both slavery and afterward as a daring leader of the Underground Railroad: that an inordinate amount of personal courage and strength of mind were required to not only persevere against the odds in life, but also to excel and be successful in the end, especially in regard to bestowing the blessings of freedom to other oppressed people.

Consequently, she dreamed big when it came to the future course of her life. Claudette fantasized about becoming a physician and even the first female and black president of the United States of America. She was determined that the dark oppression of Jim Crow would not limit her ambitions and future possibilities.

Therefore, Claudette stood out from other students at Booker T. Washington High School not only because of her shining intelligence as revealed in her bright, almond-shaped eyes that sparkled when talking about Tubman and Sojourner, but also due to her mature and insightful ways derived from deep reflection. Unlike so many of her peers, this greater degree of maturity demonstrated by this studious young woman allowed her to more closely relate to the courageous men and women, who graced the pages of black history.

Yet another factor made Claudette unique and different from most of the other students at Booker T. Washington High School. Although she dressed stylishly as much as possible and kept an overall tidy and neat appearance like her female peers from Montgomery, Claudette was still very much of a country girl at heart. She had grown up poor, which was still another dark legacy of slavery. In fact, Claudette represented a paradox: she was poor but gifted because of her intelligence and strong work ethic that caused her to excel.

Claudette's powerful work ethic, that was superior to many of the male and female students who hailed from Montgomery's urban sprawl, had been born of strong family values that insisted on excellence and the fact that she had spent years on the farm in serene Pine Level. Here, she had worked hard in her daily chores when given typical farm assignments that she performed diligently.

These unique factors and despite her city-like dress and stylish appearances, including sweaters that were popular, like her female friends, Claudette was different from the majority of other students at Booker T. Washington High School and who had been raised in the segregated black neighborhoods of Montgomery.

Indeed, as noted, Claudette had left the rural environment of Pine Level and the country, but much of the country still remained deep inside her, especially a strong traditional value system, which served her well in high school. She was not only thoroughly familiar with farm work and country life in general, but she also loved country people—their honesty and old-fashioned values that she respected and embraced for herself as a moral model—, including eating dinner from what they had grown with their own hands on the land. In addition, Claudette had basked in the open spaces and fresh air of the rural countryside far from Montgomery.

Significantly, Claudette understood how the farm and country experiences had helped to shape her in a variety of significant ways that she appreciated even more when she became older and more mature. Even the daily grind of farm chores had been invigorating and helped to make her healthier, and, more importantly, to mold her character and forge a tougher person, especially in regard to a strong work ethic and personal discipline, much more than had she remained in Montgomery.

But most of all, life in the countryside around Pine Level and on the farm far from most whites and their harsh Jim Crow world provided Claudette with a greater sense of freedom, a simple dignity gained from hard work, and a greater can-do attitude and spirit that stemmed from a pristine rural environment still untarnished by the finer things of so-called modern civilization, and a strong work ethic that was often lacking in the black urbanites of Montgomery.

Because of these past rural and farm experiences northwest of the state capital, Claudette was different from her peers from the urban environment of Montgomery. Therefore, she retained a strong personal sense of independence and the essence of a rural freedom and resourcefulness. And even while living in Montgomery's poorest neighborhood at King Hill, the beauties of nature still stirred her soul, making her reflective about both God and nature, because she knew that they were one in the same.

These admirable qualities never left the heart and soul of Claudette Colvin when living in Montgomery amid the faster-flow of life in the state capital located on the muddy Alabama River. In many ways, therefore, Claudette still viewed Montgomery very much through a rural lens although she had left the country long ago, which reflected vastly different values about life in general.

In this regard and as a very religious young woman, she saw the large urban environment of Montgomery, with its flourishing bars, gambling dens, and houses of prostitution as a corruptive environment that was unseen in the more idyllic world of Pine Level. Her harsh view of city life was especially the case with Montgomery's omnipresent of Jim Crow racist and its strict legal enforcements of the city and state segregation laws, including on the city buses that Claudette rode back and forth from King Hill to Booker T. Washington High School.

And beyond all these factors, what was most different of all about Montgomery to this smart young woman that mocked the more pristine environment of Pine Level and the world of nature that God had created and made beautiful was the white man's arbitrary—which was certainly not part of God's world in Claudette's eyes and opinion—racist oppression and rule with an iron fist.

As a lover of God and with daily life consumed by her faith, she instinctively knew that Jim Crow racism made no sense whatsoever and was not morally right in God's eyes, because the Holy Bible had taught her that everyone, black and white, was equal and they were all of God's children.

Therefore, it was elementary to Claudette's heart and mind that all of God's children were deserving of fair and equal treatment—the antithesis of the racial thinking of many whites, including those who, ironically, faithfully worshiped every Sunday and said heartfelt prayers every night. Instead, what she discovered in Montgomery was that the harshest racial laws were upheld by the law enforcement, the Alabama governor at the Governor's Mansion, and the popular white mayor: insidious racial laws of Jim Crow segregation that even leading Nazi leaders had rejected during the 1930s for employment against the Jewish people, because they considered too severe for Germany.

As noted, a farm and rural environment had created a more independent-minded, self-sufficient, resourceful, and mentally-stronger individual than if she had stayed in oppressive environment of Montgomery, where Jim Crow's harshness early battered black egos and souls in the most insidious ways and without mercy.

As the most dramatic event of Claudette's life on March 2, 1955 eventually demonstrated in full and thanks partly to the cruelties of strict Jim Crow laws, Claudette began to view her former life on the farm and living in a freer rural environment as symbolic with a sense of freedom far from the urban environment of the state capital.

Claudette dual farm and rural experiences at Pine Level had left a deep impression and permanent imprint on her heart and soul. Claudette began to see that nothing in the world of nature or in the rural environment resembled the urban world of Jim Crow that thrived in the state capital.

This intolerable situation provided her with more insight that white racism was nothing more than only a perverse facade and artificial manmade creation that simply was not on God's natural world. Therefore, she knew that this legalized racism had never been part of God's masterplan or grand design to designate only one people for seemingly endless abuse and torment for no apparent reason at all.

Blessed with an inquisitive mind, Claudette also increasingly began to question why black adults, both men and women, so easily accepted the nightmare of their Jim Crow world without ever resisting or fighting back against the harsh system of gross injustice that had made their lives so miserable as long as they could remember.

Consequently, two distinct factors from the past had combined—an uncorrupted, if not somewhat idyllic, way of life in the country and a pure love of black history and its heroes and heroines—far from Montgomery's negative environment to play a key role in setting the stage for Claudette Colvin to eventually embrace a more proactive and defiant stance against what she knew was morally wrong and entirely against God's will.

Slowly but surely, she evolved toward the ever-dangerous realm of outright resistance to the artificial dictates and harsh racial realities, which had made generations of black lives so miserable for no other reason than the single, arbitrary factor of skin color: the genesis of the making of an early Civil Rights pioneer and heroine.

In time and most importantly, Claudette's embrace of a revolutionary stance and defiant action in Montgomery on March 2, 1955 helped to pave the way for the rise of not only Rosa Parks as an ironic heroine, but also Dr. Martin Luther King, who led the Civil Rights Movement with dynamic leadership skills until his assassination, to herald a new day for America and African Americans in general.

Clearly, Claudette was as much of a starry-eyed dreamer in her early years as at age fifteen, but she was also a doer and her dreams were now more tangible, because she was determined to turn her egalitarian dreams into reality. Even more, she was also a idealistic visionary whose lofty dreams were based on the kind of personal achievements that other black women, such as Harriet Tubman and Sojourner Truth, succeeded in accomplishing and what others universally believed were well beyond their capabilities.

By remaining positive and believing in herself and the will of a benevolent God, Claudette was fully convinced that anything was possible, as if the harsh world of Jim Crow simply no longer existed to oppress her and her people: a rather remarkable development and rare insight given the ugly realities of black life in oppressive Montgomery.

After all, had not Tubman and Truth bravely struggled year after year in helping to ensure the death of America's greatest curse and most insidious institution, slavery. This commitment to proactive action in a physical sense was especially the case of Tubman, who allowed her heroic actions to speak for themselves. If she had not demonstrated personal initiative, resourcefulness, and bravery year after year, including to have escaped slavery in 1849, then she would never have become the liberator of so many of her people from slavery's horrors.

Therefore, with Tubman serving as her primary idol and source of inspiration, Claudette never stopped dreaming. By the time high school at Booker T. Washington, she finally settled on the greater goal of becoming a physician to escape the poverty of King Hill forever, despite all of the Jim Crow barriers and obstacles that were almost too many to count. Significantly and to her credit, Claudette posed no limitations on what she could accomplish in life, just like the courageous women who she had long idolized, Tubman and Truth.

This young and modest King Hill resident envisioned the great things that she might accomplish in the future, while her female classmates of her same age were primarily focused on getting the attentions of the cutest boy in class or the leading football star, or how to look whiter—all the popular rage, especially the troublesome chore of daily straightening black hair to create what was called "good hair," because of the brainwashing by white culture in regard to distorted white standards of beauty.

Besides her lofty dreams and studious nature that made her stand apart from her less ambitious and visionary peers, Claudette was still a typical high school girl, who loved to dance to the latest popular songs with her friends. As mentioned and despite a bookworm, she possessed a distinct sense of style. Wearing the nicest clothing that she either owned or borrowed, Claudette made sure that her colors matched, including a special fondness for the color blue.

However, compared to her peers, Claudette more deeply absorbed the timeless lessons, especially moral ones, that she learned from the Holy Bible and black history, especially the amazing life of Harriet Tubman. For Claudette, making mostly A's in school, especially in black history, was as automatic as it was easy for her to the amazement of her fellow students at Booker T. Washington.

All the while at school in February 1955, the heroic memory and legacies of Tubman made Claudette more self-aware of the urgent need to try to do anything in attempting to eliminate the gross injustices and racial discrimination that existed all around her, and that were an omnipresent feature of life in Montgomery for black citizens of all ages. Blacks and whites were segregated everywhere in the state capital's restaurants, water foundations, theaters, and even the graveyards based upon the harsh dictates of Jim Crow laws.

Nevertheless and despite the stiff odds for the possibility of aspiring higher in life on day in the future, Claudette continued to believe that anything was possible and that she could eventually become a player in the long-belated social change needed to uplift the long-oppressed black people of Montgomery—a direct legacy gained from her historical study of Tubman and Truth.

In this sense, Claudette began to believe that African Americans were on the verge of a new day of equality and a new birth of freedom, because she believed in her heart and soul that it was time for significant changes, and someone needed to take a defiant stand against the injustice.

For such reasons and with a greater sense of pride in Africa, black heroes and heroines, especially Harriet Tubman, and African culture in general, Claudette had herself been significantly changed by this time. In fact by early March 1955, she had been transformed into a young radical and a proud black nationalist at only age fifteen—something that was practically unheard of in ever-oppressive Montgomery, because it was a very dangerous attitude since it was both enlightening and liberating for blacks.

Because she knew that a dramatic change was needed in Montgomery and in the Deep South in general, Claudette leaned ever-closer to doing the unthinkable in the Jim Crow South—standing up and taking a defiant stand in the name of justice for all and doing something meaningful in the name of equality and justice and in all places, Montgomery.

By this time, the surreal and insurmountable horrors of Jim Crow racism and its total acceptance by an entire people had become completely intolerable to Claudette, fueling a righteous rage that burned deep inside her soul. In steadily growing stronger in mind, faith, and personal commitment, she was developing the inner strength of will and determination, which she had boldly decided would be inevitably directed in audaciously attempting to change the Jim Crow world that had destroyed the lives of so many African Americans for so long, because of its inherent criminality and insidiousness.

Most importantly, a bright, new day had dawned in the heart and soul of young Claudette Colvin because she felt a sense of liberation like Harriet Tubman. This slim and unimposing fifteen-year-old schoolgirl knew that she had to made her own personal stand and fight against racial oppression, ensuring that change was in the air because it was so long overdue. Even the spring-like weather and sunny skies over Montgomery in early March seemed to herald a new day dawning.

In her own words which revealed that Claudette could no longer tolerate racial injustices as in the past at the tender age of fifteen, although still a shy, modest, and retiring person, but she had been developed the strong attitude and instincts of an activist for justice from the forge of so many past bitter experiences and disappointments in life rooted in Jim Crow racism: "I was done talking [to her friends] about 'good hair' [or straight white hair] and 'good skin' but not addressing our grievances. I was tired of adults complaining about how badly they were treated and not doing anything about it. I'd had enough of just feeling angry about Jeremiah Reeves. I was tired of hoping for justice. When my moment came [in early March 1955], I was ready."

In the spring-like weather of late winter in Montgomery, the feeling of great change in the air invigorated Claudette Colvin, which made her believe that anything was now possible, despite too many obstacles to count in her Jim Crow world.

Chapter III

A Rendezvous with Destiny on March 2, 1955

Clearly, the heroic legacy and true meaning of Harriet Tubman's contributions to black history were still very much with Claudette on Wednesday March 2, 1955, because she so greatly admired this former slave's courage and moral integrity at a time when very few African American women were revered in the annals of American history.

This particular Wednesday in early March was the ninth Wednesday of the year, and nothing at all seemed to distinguish it from any other of the previous nine Wednesday's on this year during the administration of President Dwight David Eisenhower, America's primary hero of the Second World War. As fate would have, classes at Booker T. Washington High School ended early on this Wednesday of March 2 because of a teachers' meeting.

For a host of valid reasons, Tubman continued to serve as the most inspirational model to Claudette both in and outside of school. She closely identified with Harriet, the dynamic Eastern Shore, Maryland, heroine who had become part of her heart and soul and her very being because of the two most oppressive systems in American history that had much in common: Tubman's world of slavery and Claudette's own world of Jim Crow, which were both part of the South.

From her careful readings of the Holy Bible, Claudette knew that the racial discrimination and intolerance of Jim Crow went against God's commandants and will, which gave her the strength to face and fight evil. Like the nightmare of slavery that had long cursed America, Jim Crow was an immoral system that abused and corrupted black souls as Claudette was cruelly reminded everyday of living in Montgomery.

The historical legacies that had been reinforced to Claudette during the recent black history month of February 1955 were still very much with her in early March. Like other students, she had spent the entire month in intently studying a wide variety of distinguished chapters of African American history, including African history, which had become the special focus of her gifted teachers, especially Geraldine Nesbitt.

To Claudette, the second day of March 1955 seemed just like a typical day in Montgomery. It was an average Wednesday, the 9th one of the year and the 61st day of the year. This warm, invigorating Wednesday seemed so ordinary for African Americans trapped in Montgomery's apartheid system of Jim Crow that no black person, especially the silent older generations that had long been cowed and intimidated by seemingly endless injustices, seemed hardly to notice or care. One exception to this sad and tragic situation was Claudette Colvin. Indeed, this was no ordinary day and Claudette was no ordinary teenager, as upcoming dramatic events were about to demonstrate in full.

As noted, Classes at Booker T. Montgomery High School had been let early out for the day, and Claudette regretted to leave early on this early Wednesday afternoon that almost seemed like summer, because of her deep love for learning, especially the study of fascinating chapters of black history. But, as the same time, she wanted to see home and family and friends on King Hill during this still warming Wednesday.

Claudette, consequently, felt good about going home to see her loved ones like any fifteen-year-old schoolgirl. Now she could release her tension and joy by dancing to the latest popular Blues song, perhaps sung by B. B. King when playing in guitar "Lucille," with her friends to leave her concerns and cares behind.

Slim, pretty, and slight, Claudette now wore a pair of dark-rimmed glasses that were a bit large and stylish blue dress on her way home after a long day at school. She certainly looked studious and a bit naïve, but still she appeared somewhat older than her fifteen years. All kinds of books, especially history books, meant a great deal to Claudette, because of her love of learning that had made her one of the best students at Booker T. Washington.

As noted, she excelled in this insular black environment of King Hill and Montgomery. Claudette was blessed with a strong work ethic and lofty ambitions in which she believed anything was possible for her to achieve in life like Harriet Tubman, who had never limited her broad horizons, despite the seemingly insurmountable obstacles and limitations.

However, before Claudette could reach home in the impoverished black section of town known as "the Hill," or King Hill, in northwest Montgomery, she must once again face the mean-spirited world of Jim Crow, which had long crushed the spirit of generations of African Americans: an especially tiresome, humiliating, and irritating experience, to say the least, to Claudette.

To reach her modest, but loving, home in King Hill, she and her girlfriends, who were all carrying their heavy loads of school books from school in southeast Montgomery, would have to wait at the bus stop for the Highland Gardens bus at the intersection of Bainbridge Street and Dexter Avenue in north Montgomery.

This bus stop was located just east of the Alabama River and almost directly north of Alabama State University, which Claudette had finally concluded that she could never attend because of the lack of finances and connections.

As every other school day, this small group of black schoolgirls planned to take the bus—not a traditional yellow school bus but one that was part of Montgomery's public transportation, the City Lines bus—for the five-block trip northwest to the socially comfortable confines of King Hill. Ironically, Montgomery's whites incorrectly viewed King Hill, the poorest black neighborhood, as a dangerous and crime-ridden place in keeping with white stereotypes. In truth, the King Hill community was full of children, pets, and loving people, who supported each other like an extended kinship group in the African American tradition that dated back to the days of slavery.

Like everything else, including water fountains, restaurants, movie theaters, churches, and even graveyards, in Montgomery and the Deep South, the City Lines' buses were segregated. And this strictly-enforced segregation—the strict law of the land—was exceptionally harsh and unforgiving, regardless of age or sex.

Blacks, especially members of the older generation, had been long conditioned to do nothing that might violate the state and city (not national) laws of segregation, because the personal price that had to be paid could be very high for transgressors: arrests, fines, jail time, beatings, house burnings, and perhaps even death, including for courageous black men of God.

Discriminated against to regulate them to second class status in overall economic, political and social terms which permanently confined African Americans to the depths of society's lower order, the vast majority of Montgomery's lower class blacks could not afford cars to ensure their total dependence upon the city's buses, which faithfully carried Jim Crow with them like a cancer.

Naturally according to Jim Crow dictates enshrined in city and state laws, whites received the best seats in the front of the bus only because of their color, while blacks were forced to sit in the back, because that was the inequitable world of Montgomery and the South.

When the bus became too crowded, then blacks were forced by strict Jim Crow laws of the city of Montgomery to give up their seats to allow white customers to sit and immediately move to the back of the bus and then stand if no empty seats were available, after a weary day of work. The entire inequitable experience for African Americans on the city buses of Montgomery was as insulting as it was degrading on a daily basis in coming and going back to the black part of this segregated town, as it was meant to be from the beginning by white racist lawmakers. For Claudette, this entire unfair and inequitable situation of an open, in-your-face form of racial discrimination was not only frustrating and vexing, but also infuriating.

Like Claudette, the entire black community felt the same sense of deep outrage at the excessive injustice, but also suffered in a stoic silence like persecuted Christians under the oppressive rule of ancient Romans. Because almost all black adults worked in white Montgomery in domestic roles—mostly maids or baby sitters for women and lawn keepers and yard work for males in working for white families—, adult workers needed public transportation on a daily basis for transferring from the black part of town to the white part and then back home again at day's end.

Of course, outraged African Americans naturally complained in private to family members and friends about the gross racial injustice that was all around them to make their lives miserable. However, they simply could not do so in public because of the inherent risks involved and inevitable repercussions of an ugly nature from vigilante whites.

Even at her young age that revealed an exceptionally strong moral bearings and maturity beyond her years, Claudette detested such extreme degrees of racial discrimination and submission that had been endured in silent anguish by successive generations of adults, including her own parents and grandparents. She privately seethed at the ugly racial reality that everyone, especially adults since she was only age fifteen, remained submissive and docile, confirming to some of the ugliest stereotypes about blacks that had existed since before the Civil War.

Consequently, Claudette had long ago sworn to herself that she would never became a lowly domestic worker in a white Montgomery home for the rest of her life, like so many other black women not only in the state capital, but also across the Deep South. To her great credit during the dark, tragic days of Jim Crow, this was a sacred personal vow that she had made to herself in private and one that Claudette kept for the rest of her life.

With the increasingly powerful personal convictions of a strong mind and still inspired by the recent heroic stories about Harriet Tubman and Sojourner Truth that she had so thoroughly absorbed like a sponge throughout the glorious February as part of Black History Month, meanwhile, Claudette and her best friends from her class waited patiently for the arrival of the city bus at the bus stop at Dexter Avenue and Bainbridge Street.

Here, in high spirits after having been let out of school early, they talked about classes and typical teenage topics like grades and cute boys just before the Highland Gardens bus arrived to take them back to King Hill. As mentioned, what was most remarkable about this day, March 2, 1955, was absolutely nothing of any distinction whatsoever. It was just another day and part of the normal, if not somewhat boring, routine for Claudette.

In fact and in every way, this Wednesday, or "hump day," was too ordinary in its routine predictability and lack of uniqueness of any kind. However, as countless times in the past, history was about to be made when least expected.

The Arrival of a Bus

In fact and entirely unknown to Claudette Colvin at this time, March 2, 1955 was about to become one of the most remarkable of days and one that was about to spark not only the Montgomery Bus Boycott, but also the Civil Rights Movement in the end—one the greatest of all people's movements for significant social change in United States history by forcing America to live-up to its lofty egalitarian promises, as enshrined in the Declaration of Independence, of equality for all of its citizens.

Symbolically and significantly in overall historical terms, the Montgomery Bus Boycott actually had its distinctive people's protest roots in colonial American's massive boycott of British imported goods that paved the way to open conflict and the American Revolution—a great and popular egalitarian tradition of America even before the official establishment of the United States on July 4, 1776.

Indeed, quite simply, neither Claudette Colvin or the United States of America would ever be the same after the hot afternoon of March 2, 1955, for what was about to transpire, when the bus suddenly arrived at the bus stop and she boarded with her female friends like so often in the past for the return trip home to the poorest part of town, King Hill.

When Claudette first stepped—a fateful step but a most historic one because of what was about to happen—aboard the Highlands Gardens bus, she and her female friends, a group of chatting high school students, paid with a pink-colored student coupon for a half fare of five cents as usual for the short ride of only five blocks back home. Overburdened with the weight of their schoolbooks, taking the bus was absolutely necessary for Claudette and her four female friends, thanks to the cheap price due to the student discount. Of course, like the rest of Montgomery, including Claudette's high school, and the Deep South, the bus ride was made less than enjoyable because it was a segregated one in the Jim Crow tradition.

After walking past the first rows of seats of the bus that were marked "white," Claudette and one of her female friends found a seat on the left side around the middle row half-way to the rear of the seating section, that separated black from white, because the bus was not crowded on this sunny Wednesday.

Claudette sat down into the window seat, and she almost immediately gazed out at familiar urban sights of southeast Montgomery. Meanwhile, the two other black students sat in the same row on the right side of the bus.

Because the afternoon was hot and the books burdensome, Claudette and her friend sitting beside her felt a sense of relief. They felt invigorated by no longer carrying the books that were now placed in their laps, while conversing with each other about whatever was on their minds, after having been released early from school. And, of course, meeting any kind of trouble with white rules and authority was the last thing on the minds of these young black students, including Claudette.

At this time while looking out the window and becoming silent and reflective, Claudette thought about Harriet Tubman, who had been a lowly slave on Maryland's Eastern Shore, before rising to greatness by her own initiative and courage against seemingly impossible odds. The distinguished legacy of this remarkable woman as the consummate freedom fighter and heroine before and during the Civil War was still alive deep the soul of Claudette Colvin.

This young student and lover of black history from the small house on King Hill perhaps remembered Tubman's inspiring words about having become a leading conductor of the Underground Railroad, when leading so many of her people north to freedom by following the bright light of the North Star, which always pointed to the Promised Land: "I did not take up this work for my own benefit, but for those of my race who need help."

Then, after the Civil War and the destruction of slavery, Tubman nobly continued the fight for equality for not only blacks, but also for women's rights. Clearly, like Claudette Colvin, Tubman was an amazing and dynamic woman ahead of her time. Both of these thoughtful and socially conscious black women turned their sights on destroying the most evil institutions of their day.

Even more, this slight Maryland woman, who was as dark as Claudette without any hint of white blood, of a feisty and God-fearing nature, was known far and wide as "the Black Moses" by the time of the Civil War. And like Tubman who believed that God protected her during her dangerous missions to rescue slaves, including her own parents and siblings, Claudette was a devout young woman. At all times, she placed her faith in God and the Holy Bible like when Harriet had performed her risky missions back and forth from the Eastern Shore of Maryland in the blighted land of slavery.

Therefore, for such reasons, Claudette never forgot Tubman's heroic actions or her stirring words about the primary guiding light in her life: "I felt like Moses [because] De Lord tole me to do dis." With God on her side and traveling with her in protective fashion through one danger after another, Tubman led a heroic life in the face of seemingly insurmountable odds, especially in rescuing scores of slaves from their greatest horror on Maryland's Eastern Shore.

Year after year throughout the 1850s, Tubman constantly risked capture and death as a primary leader of the Underground Railroad, having too many close calls to count in doing God's work. But she never faltered during these great trials of endurance and faith, serving her people and living by her own personal credo: "For no man should take me alive; I should fight for my liberty as long as my strength lasted" in this life.

Claudette had long taken such inspiring words of her historical idol to heart. And she now held these sacred words of the incomparable Harriet Tubman dear even after having taken her seat on the City Lines Bus that was going to take her back home to King Hill. Like Tubman who explained the depth of her religious faith, "I jest asked Jesus to take keer of me," so Claudette believed that God was now with and beside her this afternoon on the bus. In fact, Claudette believed that she had three protective and benevolent companions with her on March 2, Jesus Christ, Harriet Tubman, and Sojourner Truth.

Indeed, all the time that she was sitting on the city bus for the relatively short ride home and minding her own business, the spirit and freedom-loving ways of these three defiant rebels against abusive authority of the unrighteous, including evil itself, was very much in the heart and mind of Claudette on the segregated bus.

All in all, this nondescript city bus plying Montgomery's streets now served as a microcosm of the unjustness of Jim Crow, where blacks and whites were kept segregated for abstract reasons that made no logical sense in the young, but mature, mind of Claudette, especially in overall religious terms.

All throughout the month of February and as mentioned, she had been reminded of the courage and audacity of heroines Harriet Tubman and Sojourner Truth, as she had been taught by the passionate teachers at Booker T. Washington High School. And she would never forget the invaluable life lessons that she had learned from studying black history.

To compensate for the battered minds and souls of young blacks by the racial Apartheid system that so seriously wrecked healthy egos and undermined self-images, including young women like Claudette, during their formative years, Black History Month had acted like a soothing tonic that was most inspirational, if not healing.

Well-educated black teachers, mostly women, were extremely proud of the heroic story of their people, who had been so much of America's story—beginning in Jamestown, Virginia, in 1616, from the beginning, and they had presented the distinguished part of blacks in America's stirring saga. Consequently, these gifted teachers had directed a keen focus on the courage of distinguished black heroes and heroines from a storied past and specifically for students like Claudette.

In some ways, it now seemed almost as if fate, history, and the present time had placed young Claudette in a most vexing situation and in the ultimate personal dilemma, which she had long detested and had no solution. Almost like a stake driven into Claudette's heart, Montgomery's oppressive Jim Crow world had been hell on earth for generations of African Americans, and she was now no less a victim as she fully realized.

At this time, seemingly countless racial injustices had fueled a smoldering rage that existed just below the surface of black men and women, including Claudette, whose psyches had been long beaten-up by the artificial and cruel dictates of an unrestrained racism, which seemed to have no end because it was the law of the land.

This harsh, unforgiving racial environment that could not have been more unjust to mock both the Declaration of Independence and the United States Constitution—the unsettling, if not sickening, realities that were well understood by Claudette Colvin—was no accident. It had been artificially created by white lawmakers for the express purpose of denying blacks equality to create a permanent underclass, which could then be exploited and abused to the dominant social, political, and economic systems.

This legalized Apartheid system of Alabama and the Deep South was insidious, and calculated to also crush the dreams, hopes, and ambitions of generations of African Americans for nothing more than because they possessed darker skins. But Claudette Colvin determined that this soul-shattering environment of Jim Crow would never destroy her great dream of becoming a fully-rounded person and future physician: a lofty ambition for a young black woman in the Deep South during the dark days of Jim Crow.

Quite the contrary and like her historical mentors Harriet Tubman and Sojourner Truth, Claudette embraced the fiery spirit of rebellion and a quiet righteous rage against racial injustice because of the omnipresent discrimination and oppression that had no end, including on the city bus. The daily experience of experiencing black shame and humiliation in riding the bus was just accepted as a normal part of the dark legacy of oppression like the rising and setting of the sun: just another degrading experience and one of so many such indignities in the lives of Montgomery's black residents of all ages and sexes.

In her own heart and mind, Claudette had already become a rebel by this time. Especially after the Jeremiah Reeves tragedy, she was already angry and defiant toward the unfairness of the whole inequitable status quo and the dominant oppression of Jim Crown in a tortured land that was more the home of the unjust rather than "of the brave," as emphasized in the national anthem with so much national pride.

But the nightmare of legalized discrimination across the Deep South ensured that this was not the land of the brave, mocking the core meaning of the United States Constitution to an extreme degree. In general, whites in the South proved to be cowardly for faithfully, if not enthusiastically, clinging to the unjustness of Jim Crow like their lives depended upon it to reduce their moral authority and overall standing, especially in the eyes of God, while blacks could be seen as almost cowardly—actually cowed and browbeaten—for accepting the endless abuse in silence.

Therefore, despite only age fifteen, in her thoughtful and mature realizations about life and race that were so closely intertwined with overt oppression in Montgomery, this young woman from King Hill already viewed black and white adults with a measure of contempt, because an especially ugly racism had made both look equally bad in Claudette's eyes and the eyes of God. She felt deep disgust that no one was making a stand against what Claudette knew was the epitome of evil.

In the mountains of a beautiful Galilee in today's northern Israel as Claudette knew from her daily readings of the Holy Bible, Jesus Christ had preached the faith of freedom and equality for all his children, regardless of class, race, or color. Only man himself had so grossly perverted God's sacred laws and selfishly bent his will on earth to create the hideous situation that now thrived in Montgomery to damage the souls of both black and white people, but for entirely different reasons.

Therefore, although not fully realized at this time by her in regard to its potential explosiveness, Claudette was almost like a smoldering power keg that was now highly combustible, because of the merger of a lifetime of abuse under Jim Crow oppression that had fused with the glories of a heroic black past, especially in regard to the dual heroines of Tubman and Truth. In this sense, the past and present had already emerged in an unique way inside the heart and soul of Claudette Colvin by the time that she had boarded the city bus in a routine and nonchalant manner that gave no hint of a new attitude.

What had also combined with this novel combustible mix was Claudette's realization that she had been fated to be among the members of the lowest member of American society in the land of Jim Crow because of her youth, sex, and color—of course, all ugly and unfair realities that were well beyond her control, while she had long suffered in a stoic silence, like every black person in Montgomery, and felt trapped in the living daily nightmare of her Deep South world.

The Inspirational, Omnipresent Spirit of Harriet Tubman

Beyond all doubt and in Claudette's own words, the personally-liberating spirit of Harriet Tubman was certainly beside this studious black teenager at this time, while she sat on the bus with her friend without a care in the world. Of course, the best proof of this reality was the simple fact that what was about to happen and play out in full on this segregated bus was nothing less than a great test of personal and moral courage and content of character for Claudette—a defiant confrontation with Jim Crow.

And, most importantly, this upcoming confrontation of Claudette with the evils of Jim Crow was destined to be a supreme moral test on a level and scale not seen in Montgomery in many years. In fact, nothing like this upcoming moral and righteous act of defiance as orchestrated by Claudette had ever taken place on a Montgomery bus.

Indeed, Claudette's act of conscience and forthcoming defiance against Jim Crow's injustices and abusive white authority was destined to change the life of this young woman forever. It is not known but perhaps while sitting in history class at Booker T. Washington High School, Claudette might have recently wondered at some point what it would have been like if she had been a slave in Alabama—like her own ancestors in the heart of cotton country—long ago, because of the in-depth teachings of her history instructors, especially her favorite teacher Geraldine Nesbitt. She possessed some white blood unlike Colvin, but never allowed her white side to intervene with her passion for black history and her own personal desire to fight against racial injustice.

It is not known when under history's sway, but Claudette might have imagined in her daydreaming at some point that she had been a Maryland slave who had escaped slavery with the fearless "Black Moses" leading the way north and out of bondage in the Upper South's "Egypt" like the ancient Hebrew people. After, the ancient Jews had followed their revered prophet Moses in leading the way to the "New Canaan" that had been promised by God, and now African Americans needed a comparable deliverance from evil.

For such reasons and because of what was about to happen on the bus and based on Claudette's own words, the fiery attitude and indestructible spirit of Harriet Tubman was definitely with her on the hot afternoon of fateful March 2, 1955. Indeed, under circumstances that are unimaginable today to Americans, Claudette was about to commit an incredibly brave act of almost unbelievable moral courage and outright defiance to white injustice in the most impossible of situations.

Indeed, despite only age fifteen, from the wrong size of the tracks, and of a small size compared to most of her schoolmates, Claudette was about to challenge <u>on her own</u> the entire system of Jim Crow that had been created on the premise of black inferiority that served as the very foundation of the white Apartheid rule and autocratic authority—a most daunting and serious undertaking never before seen in Montgomery from a fifteen-year-old black school girl or anyone else for that matter.

What has been most forgotten about the leading factor that sparked a heightened sense of indignation, outrage, and feisty fighting spirit in this quiet and shy lover of black history was the inspirational legacy and never-say-die qualities of Harriet Tubman. For such reasons, the native Marylander and former slave had become a legend to the northern abolitionist community, which was centered in Boston, Massachusetts, by the time of the Civil War. In fact, Tubman emerged as the foremost black heroine during the Civil War—America's Iliad.

At this time after not long boarding the bus, taking a seat, and talking to her friend, the fifteen-year-old Claudette could never have possibly imagined at this time that she was about to trigger the very beginning of America's most powerful and influential people's movement that initiated the most significant social change during the twentieth century—the Montgomery Bus Boycott that then sparked the Civil Rights Movement that changed the lives of black people and the world—by her open act of defiance and courage, which broke all the unjust racial rules that had been insidiously constructed by Jim Crow.

As fate would have it and as was expected, Claudette's bus gradually began to take on more passengers coming home from work. These new arrivals were mostly whites who had just left work from downtown Montgomery's department stores (Rosa Parks now worked in one as a seamstress), shops, and state government workplaces, while the afternoon heat increased on this sunny Wednesday. There was no air conditioning on the increasingly-crowded bus to ease the heat and rising humidity that almost felt like the steamy days of blistering July, and the additional number of people made it seem hotter on an early March day.

Slowly but surely, the front rows of white seats were gradually filled, and some black passengers now stood in the wide aisle and held onto the metal poles at the edge of aisles, after having vacated their seats to whites. Suddenly, while still sitting in the window seat, Claudette noticed a mature white woman standing by her aisle in anticipation that she and her friend would shortly be vacating the entire row and move toward the rear of the bus, so that she could take a seat: the sudden development that was required by law which always guaranteed an immediate response and a most submissive one.

As everyone in Montgomery and on the crowded city bus fully expected in this situation, Claudette's friend dutifully departed her seat. She then routinely walked to the back of the bus without thinking in an automatic response to obey the laws and rules of the city and state. But Claudette had something not only different but also very special on her mind by this time. At this time on the verge of open confrontation, she was not thinking about the bus, the white woman standing in the aisle and automatically expecting her seat, or the existing delicate racial situation, but about the heroics of Harriet Tubman in the past, when expectations for black women had never been lower.

And when the white driver suddenly shouted, "I need those seats" on the crowded bus, Claudette remained seated and silent in her stoic moral stance like the black Madonna of Catholic and Orthodox counties, including Poland and Russia.

At this moment, she did not think about the automatic racial expectations of the standing white woman, who was around age forty, or the angry white driver, who the city had legally empowered with police powers to deal with black passengers, who did not follow his orders: directives that were entirely backed-up by the city and segregation rules and laws based on the racism of Jim Crow. In her stillness and seemingly peace of mind while remaining in her seat without saying a word, Claudette ignored it all. She simply remained sitting in her seat as if in a deep state of Buddha-like meditation before an ancient sacred shrine in the Far East.

At this time, Claudette only thought about the daring deeds and sacrifices of Harriet Tubman and Sojourner Truth in battling the evils of slavery, and what they had accomplished against the rules and all expectations for lowly black women of allegedly no worth whatsoever. Claudette wondered what would these two remarkably strong and life-long crusading black women, whose religious faith had guided them to greatness year after year, had done under comparable circumstances, especially because Jim Crow was only a milder form of slavery? What would these two defiant and courageous women do in this oppressive situation? How had they confronted and overcome the horrors of slavery and still persevered in the end to emerge as heroines? What Claudette already knew was that fact that they had fought against a legally institution protected in the United States Constitution and the law of the land, slavery.

Almost without thinking or reflecting in an instinctive, if not automatic, response, Claudette already knew the answer to these intriguing questions that quickly flashed through her mind, while the racial showdown on the bus was gradually becoming more tense to quickly reach the point of no return. And the unequivocal answer to these questions had emerged from the depths of her heart and soul to reveal the full content of her character and faith.

Seemingly almost without exactly knowing how or why, she possessed no fear in this dangerous situation that was steadily escalating, but only a calm reassurance and quiet confidence in a serene righteousness. Almost as if she was at some other place in the past, Claudette felt that Tubman and Sojourner were now by her side to face whatever trial that would inevitably come.

In overall moral terms and feeling that she had no choice, Claudette now realized what she had to do under the circumstances that was unprecedented in Montgomery: ironically, simply doing nothing at all by remaining quietly and peacefully in her seat in violating the entrenched racist laws, which was the most revolutionary and militant act that she could do in this situation and one that was about to shock both the white and black communities of Montgomery like no single event in recent memory.

For such reasons at this moment of crisis on the crowded bus, "history had me glued to the seat," as Claudette explained her overall situation and the mysterious nature of the mystical force that had primarily kept her from moving an inch, because of her own stubborn will that was fueled by a righteous rage.

Indeed, in her own words, "emotionally, I felt as though Harriet Tubman's hands were pushing me down on one shoulder and Sojourner Truth was pushing me down on the other. From these historical, iconic women I had been taught so much about, I just couldn't move."

Even in this increasingly tense situation on the quiet bus that even might turn into a case of risking her life because of violent retaliation, Claudette never lost her keen sense of humanity and fair play. As Claudette late explained what she was now thinking even while she was boldly openly defying white authority and breaking all the racist rules at great risk to herself: "I might have considered getting up if the woman had been elderly, but she wasn't [and although the] other three black girls in my row got up and moved back, but I didn't. I just couldn't."

Clearly, this was the supreme moment of truth for Claudette Colvin, and she, Montgomery, African Americans, and the South would never be the same, because of what was happening—an entirely spontaneous and natural act without premeditation or plan, but one based solidly on fundamental moral truths. All the while, the standing white woman in the bus aisle would not take the seat that had been just vacated by Claudette's female friend, because the entire row had to be black free, before any white person dared to sit down.

And, of course, this development was not now possible because Claudette remained sitting in her seat, while not saying a word: all on the Jim Crow premise that blacks had to be seated behind whites in the segregated seating arrangement. As noted, it was the moral force of past black freedom fighters and early feminists Tubman and

Sojourner who kept Claudette firmly in place and not moving an inch.

Indeed, by this time, Claudette was thoroughly inspired by the past achievements of black heroes and heroines, who had imbued their fiery spirits and actions against injustice deep into her heart and soul. As noted, she had developed a great pride in Africa and its people that was ahead of its time, and the legacy of the distant African motherland was also playing a role in keeping her seated.

In Claudette's own words about the importance of African history and how it inspired her: "We were supposed to be ashamed of our African past. But Africa made me proud." Pride in black history and culture on both sides of the Atlantic profoundly motivated Claudette at this time, inspiring to her to act with a courage in the face of adversity seldom seen in Montgomery, especially from a female high school student.

Besides the enduring lessons of history and righteous tales from the Holy Bible, a host of harsh facts and racial realities also emboldened Claudette as never before, especially the sad fate of fellow student and friend Jeremiah Reeves. In her own words that revealed a new defiant attitude and stronger mind about the world around her: "I had been talking about revolution ever since Jeremiah Reeves."

Claudette explained another fact that now motivated and inspired her to defy the oppressive system of injustice that had abused black people for generations: "Rebellion was on my mind that day. All during February we'd been talking [at school] about people who had taken stands [the very subject that Senator John F. Kennedy had written about in his *Profiles of Courage*]. We had been studying the [United States] Constitution in Miss Nesbitt's class [and] I knew I had rights. I had paid my fare the same as white passengers . . . I was thinking, Why should I have to get up just because a [white] driver [empowered by Montgomery's racist laws and regulations] tells me to, or just became I'm black? Right then, I decided I wasn't gonna take it anymore. I hadn't planned it, but my decision was built on a lifetime of nasty experiences."

Sadly, the harsh racial experiences for Claudette extended all the way back to age four, when she had been backhanded across the mouth by an incensed white mother for daring to have only minimal interact with white children, who had initiated that contact in the first place.

"I Just Couldn't Move. History Had Me Glued to the Seat"

Now enraged by a completely unexpected defiance of a black female teenager, who dared not to obey the direct order of the white bus driver to move back to the rear, he yelled, "Why are you still sittin' there?" Claudette's stoic response continued to be a dignified and eerie quiet defiance that so loudly said everything in the strict, intolerant world of Jim Crow. In her own words: "I didn't get up, and I didn't answer him [and] It got real quiet on the bus."

All the while, the increasingly impatient and unbelieving white woman continued to stand in the center aisle across from Claudette, as the angry white driver continued to shout for the defiant teenager to immediately vacate her seat. The upset driver, Robert W. Cleere, then pulled into Court Square, which was the main downtown stop, which was located about six blocks west of the stately Alabama State Capitol of white marble and the city's largest Confederate Monument. Here, at Court Square, he called for a transit law enforcement officer to make the arrest of a young black female, who was viewed a troublemaker who certainly deserved punishment for violating scared racial laws and rules.

Ironically, this central location of Court Square, where the overall situation on the Highlands Gardens bus had reached a new level of heightened tension and seriousness, is now situated only two blocks southwest of today's Rosa Parks Library and Museum on Montgomery Street; less than two blocks directly south of today's Freedom Rides Museum on Court Street; and today's Civil Rights Memorial, which has been dedicated to the heroes and heroines of Civil Rights, located about two blocks to the southeast on Washington Avenue.

Meanwhile, at Court Square, Claudette's situation worsened in an inevitable development of an escalating white backlash in the form of angry police officers, despite her not saying a single word, while not moving and remaining in her seat by the window. When the transit officer asked her to leave her seat, Claudette still refused to depart without saying a word. The tense standoff continued unabated.

As Claudette later explained this increasingly serious situation that was already escalating beyond all control, taking a life and a momentum of its own: "I just couldn't move . . . That's the only way I know how to resist, to not move." The frustrated transit officer then explained to the driver that he lacked arrest authority.

The thwarted transit officer departed the bus in frustration and then the bus continued only a block north to reach the interaction of Commerce and Bibb Streets. Here, a police car was waiting for the arrival of the bus and to administer legal Jim Crow justice to a fifteen-year-old student. The two white Montgomery police officers—there were no blacks on the entire police force—climbed aboard the bus in full uniforms of blue and armed with deadly weapons to confront the silent and petite schoolgirl, who dared to maintain her defiant stance and human dignity in the dark heart of the Deep South.

The angry police officer, after calling her a "thing," stood over Claudette and yelled, "Aren't you going to get up?" Claudette now uttered her first words during the entire showdown, "No Sir." Now obviously angry, the police officer then yelled, "Get up!' In Claudette's words, "I started crying, but I felt even more defiant. I kept saying over and over, in my high-pitched voice, 'Its my constitutional right to sit here as much as that lady. I paid my fare, its my constitutional right!' I knew I was talking back to a white policeman, but I had had enough."

Then, the inevitable police muscle took centerstage to end the standoff of wills, when the two police officers grabbed Claudette's hands and literally pulled her up out of her seat and dragged her backwards. Jerked violently upward, Claudette never forgot how her schoolbooks "went flying everywhere [and] I went limp as a baby—I was too smart to fight back [but] They started dragging me backwards off the bus [and] One of them kicked me . . . I sure didn't fight back [while] I kept screaming over and over, 'It's my constitutional right!' . . . I was shouting out my rights."

Claudette, while "crying hard," was then roughly placed in the back seat of the police squad car at the intersection of Commerce and Bibb Streets within, most symbolically, only blocks of the first White House of the Confederacy and just north of today's Rose Parks Library and Museum. Here, she was shortly ordered to stick her hands out the police car window, and an officer shackled her hands in handcuffs, as if Claudette was a murder suspect, and now the arrest of a juvenile under the age of sixteen was official.

Then, the police car drove to the same city police station where the false confessions had been forced from the heavily-pressed teenager Jeremiah Reeves that guaranteed his future death in the electric chair by the verdict of an all-white jury, while one white officer sat by Claudette in the back seat. She was then verbally harassed and abused about her looks and blackness by Police Officers Paul Headly and Thomas J. Ward.

In her own words of the traumatic experience that additionally exposed the depth of the automatic and casual racism that thrived in Montgomery, including in the police force that ironically was dedicated to protecting all of the capital's citizens: "All ride long they swore at me and ridiculed me. They took turns trying to guess my bra size. They called me "nigger bitch" and cracked jokes about parts of my body. I recited the Lord's Prayer and the Twenty-third Psalm [entitled "The Lord the Shepherd of His People," over and over in my head":

"The Lord is my shepherd
I shall not want
He makes me to lie down in green pastures
He leads me beside the still waters

He restores my soul
He leads me in the paths of righteousness
For His name's sake

Yea, though I walk through the valley of the shadow of death
I will fear no evil
For You *are* with me;
Your rod and Your staff, they comfort me."

Finally, the police car, with Claudette and the white officer in the back seat, reached the police station after a frightening ordeal for the young girl, who was on her own.

But the most frightening events were still about to transpire for her at the police station.

As Claudette explained the harrowing experience upon entering Montgomery's main police station and not a juvenile facility where she should have been taken by the police, when she felt a rush of fear: "More [white] cops looked up when we came in and started calling me "Thing" and "Whore." They booked me and took my fingerprints. Then, they put me back in the car and drove me to the city jail—the adult jail. Someone led me straight to a cell without giving me any chance to make a phone call. He opened the door and told me to get inside. He shut it hard behind me and turned the key. The lock fell into place with a heavy sound. It was the worst sound I ever heard. It sounded final. It said I was trapped . . . I fell on my knees in the middle of the cell and started crying again. I didn't know if anyone knew [she was not allowed to even call her mother] where I was or what had happened to me. I had no idea how long I would be there. I cried and I put my hands together and prayed like I had never prayed before."

In her darkest hour, Claudette was fortified by one of her mother's favorite sayings that now especially applied to her deplorable situation that now seemed hopeless and without a solution, when she feared that she had been abandoned by everyone: "If God is for you, the Devil can't do you any harm."

A Most Timely Rescue

Fortunately, Claudette's distraught female friends on the bus raced home and immediately called Claudette's mother, Mary Ann, where she worked as a domestic in a white household in Montgomery. Friends then went to the white household to care for the three white children, while Mary Ann rushed home and called their beloved pastor, Reverend H. H. Johnson, for help.

In record time, Mary Ann and the good reverend, who fortunately owned a car, drove straight to the police station. Inside the police station, Claudette's mother became extremely upset upon seeing her tearful teenage daughter behind bars, where she had languished and cried for several hours. Reverend Johnson immediately paid the bail for Claudette's release. Then, they drove back to King Hill with a feeling of great relief and thankfulness to God because Claudette was now free, after a harrowing ordeal for the teenager.

Mary Ann simply said to her daughter in regard to her defiance and courage demonstrated on the bus: "they picked the wrong day [March 2, 1955] to pick on me." Indeed, knowing the importance of the recent lessons in black history, especially in regard to having learned more about the defiance and bravery of Harriet Tubman, Claudette concluded how, "If it had happened any other time of the year, we might have just gotten off the bus."

Here, in the poorest black section of Montgomery, already "word had spread everywhere" throughout the poor black community of King Hill, explained Claudette, and "All our neighbors came around, and they were just squeezing me to death. I felt happy and proud. I have been talking about getting our rights ever since Jeremiah Reeves was arrested, and now they knew I was serious [and] I felt proud [because] I had stood up for our rights. I had done something a lot of adults hadn't done."

Claudette's courageous actions that had defied the white bus driver, transit officer, and then two police officers, who were known for the harsh treatment of blacks, were the talk of not only the black community, but also of all Montgomery and across the United States. In a letter to Claudette, one man in Sacramento, California, penned with heartfelt admiration and respect to this young lady only age fifteen and who had demonstrated a dignified bravery, despite the odds that had been stacked so high against her: "How encouraging it would be if more adults had your courage, self-respect and integrity."

On the Sunday, March 6, 1955, Reverend H. H. Johnson led the large black congregation in solemn prayer for the young woman, who had defied white authority and Jim Crow in her own way and entirely on her own without any support from anyone else. Back at school and like other students and teachers except those who were ashamed that a fifteen-year-old classmate had been able to do on her own because they lacked the courage to do, Miss Nesbit, who admired Harriet Tubman as much as Claudette, warmly embraced her. Bestowing the ultimate compliment, the esteemed teacher exclaimed to Claudette, "You were so brave."

Branded a Criminal

In the end and based on false charges of her fighting the police officers and resisting arrest, the police department had "charged her with being a delinquent, but she was an honors student at Booker T. Washington," in the words of young, black attorney Fred M. Gray.

First and foremost, Claudette needed assistance because of her upcoming court case. She had been charged with having broken city and state segregation laws. Claudette's mother, Mary Jane, called Montgomery's most prominent defender of black rights, E. D. Nixon. He was a mature Pullman porter who possessed a gift for effective interaction and communications between black and white.

Thankfully, the tall, dignified Nixon decided to help the poor teenager from King Hill. Nixon immediately went to work, calling one of Montgomery's two black lawyers, Fred D. Gray. He was only twenty-four, ambitious, and fresh out of law school. Most of all, Gray was enthusiastic and eager for the new challenge.

Born in Montgomery, raised in the black community of Washington Park—a more advantaged neighborhood than Claudette's poorer King Hill—, a product of Alabama State College like Geraldine Nesbitt before entering the Alabama Bar Association, and destined for greatness in the Civil Rights Movement, Gray was special. He eventually became a leading Civil Rights lawyer, including the winning of widespread recognition by representing Rosa Parks and Dr. Martin Luther King in the future. Gray had dedicated his life to one goal that consumed him: "destroy everything segregated I could find." And he found plenty of opportunities in this tainted and blighted land, beginning with Claudette' case.

Attorney Gray's personal dedication and devotion mirrored that of Claudette, resulting in a natural union of two strong-willed individuals, who were devoted to bestowing freedom and making America a better place for everyone by forcing the nation to live-up to its lofty egalitarian values. Like Claudette and in his own words, he hated the fact that in "Alabama's capital city—the 'Birthplace of the Confederacy'—churches, schools, hospitals, and places of public accommodations were all segregated [and] Whites and blacks were segregation from the time they were born until the time they were buried in segregated cemeteries."

For the teenage Claudette who was without funds or much hope of mounting a successful defense because she was determined to plead not guilty during the trial, Gray was literally a savior. Most significantly, Claudette possessed the courage that ensured that she was destined to become the first and only black to have declared themselves to be not guilty—a direct challenge to the entire Jim Crow system of legalized discrimination—before a hostile white court and white judge.

As attorney Gray wrote: "I represented Claudette Colvin in the juvenile court of Montgomery County. We [Rosa Park] discussed the possibility of a boycott. I told Rosa Parks [NAACP longtime member and respected secretary of the Montgomery branch while working as a downtown department store as a seamstress], as I had told other leaders I Montgomery, that I thought the Claudette Colvin arrest was a good test case to end segregation on the buses. However, the black leadership in Montgomery at that time thought we should wait."

The Montgomery newspaper, the *Alabama Journal*, printed the story about the juvenile trial on March 19, 1955: "Claudette Colvin of 622 E. Dixon Drive [in King Hill], a bespectacled, studious looking high school student, accepted the court's ruling [of guilty, including the charge of fighting police officers and resisting arrest—which was simply not the case—and placed on probation for violating the city's segregation law] with the same cool aloofness she had maintained throughout her 2 ½ hour hearing" before [white] Judge Wiley C. Hill, Jr., of the Juvenile Court.

Ironically, more damaging to Claudette in the long-term was not this white judge's harsh and unfair decision, but a black leadership decision not to protest Claudette's conviction to trigger the bus boycott in the state capital. The decision by Montgomery's black leadership, including the NAACP, of the nascent bus boycott movement to not fully support her (because of her young age, lower class status, feistiness, and broken home background, King Hill residence in the poorest part of town, etc.), as she deserved, and only to then wait for another time to make their case against the evils of segregation, despite the fact that this young woman was the key catalyst for significant change, was final.

Therefore, Claudette Colvin was relegated to historical obscurity for decades, because the challenge to bus segregation was destined to come with Rosa Parks and not the Claudette Colvin, who defied Jim Crow segregation nearly a year earlier: developments that were all part of a carefully-calculated decision of black leadership in Montgomery.

Twenty-six years older than Claudette, Rosa Parks was the ideal face of the forthcoming mass protest movement, which became known as the Montgomery Bus Boycott: mature at age forty-two, a longtime NAACP official, light-skinned, soft-spoken, as dignified as a nun in a secluded convent, a married woman, a longtime wage earner, unemotional to a fault, quiet by inclination, and tailor-made for heroine status—the antithesis of the outspoken, feisty, and now pregnant Colvin.

In Claudette's words: "When I heard the news [that another black woman was arrested for not relinquishing her seat on the bus on December 1, 1955] that it was Rosa Parks, I had several feelings: I was glad an adult had finally stood up to the system, but I felt left out. I was thinking, Hey, I did that [9] months ago and everybody dropped me [but] I was eager to keep going in court [because] I had wanted them to keep appealing my case. I had enough self-confidence to keep going [however] they all turned their backs on me, especially after I got pregnant [and] no matter how I felt or what I thought, I wasn't going to get my chance."

But most important, it was Claudette who had been the first female protestor and boldly led the way to spark the famous Montgomery Bus Boycott. Gray described how: "Nine months before Rosa Parks refused to give up her seat I represented Claudette Colvin for a similar act of resistance [Rosa Parks and] I was still in awe of the courage that it took for a 15-year-old school girl to defy a white bus driver and white policemen, jailers, and judges just because she felt in her soul that it was wrong . . . I readily agreed to represent Claudette, thinking that this would be the chance I had been waiting on to challenge the constitutionally of Montgomery's segregation ordinances and Alabama's segregation statues."

In Gray's words in regard to the overall situation that eventually developed: "the Colvin case proved a false start as far as giving me the opportunity to challenge Alabama's segregation laws [in part because] the juvenile court of Montgomery County convicted her on all changes [and] placed her on indefinite, unsupervised probation."

Gray appealed the conviction on May 6, 1955. He managed to get two of the three charges against Claudette dropped. However, the most damaging charge of "assaulting" an officer of the law, which was a trumped-up charge like those against the doomed Jeremiah Reeves, saddled her with a permanent criminal charge.

This unfortunate fate, of course, was a primary reason that explained why Claudette was so quickly and unceremoniously abandoned—she heard from no one, including not even Rosa Parks after she was convicted of the criminal charge of assaulting a police officer—to guarantee that she was not destined to become a major player in the famous Montgomery Bus Boycott Movement, which she basically started and inspired by a single act of defiance.

This groundbreaking people's movement in the name of racial equality and justice succeeded from the sheer determination and unity of the black community in refusing to ride the city buses and because of the dynamic leadership of young Dr. Martin Luther King. Like no other black leader, Dr. King inspired his long-oppressed people, including Claudette who rejoiced in his fiery words when she heard his speeches, to peacefully protest injustice.

Devout as always, Claudette closely embraced Dr. King's powerful messages and spiritual beliefs that were the same as those of this determined teenager from the poverty of King Hill: "God is with this movement" for equality and justice in Dr. King's optimistic words of hope and faith.

Browder v. Gayle

In January 1956, Fred Gray visited the small King Hill home of Claudette's family about a new case to challenge Montgomery's and Alabama's segregation laws in the district court. Claudette was eager for the challenge and opportunity to strike another blow against legally entrenched racism and especially one so solidly entrenched in the legal system. Because Claudette was still a minor, her family had to give the go ahead and consent to Gray's initiative. They, of course, readily gave their permission for the daughter, to her delight, to forge ahead in the pursuit of justice.

Thereafter, Claudette diligently prepared for the upcoming court case like a young, aspiring lawyer, while raising her new-born infant Raymond, who was light-skinned. She recalled how at "night, while I would like in bed and rehearse the things I was going to say, Raymond slept beside me in a little bassinet. It was just the two of us in the front room . . . Sometimes I thought about Harriet Tubman, about her courage," which was still in the heart and mind of Claudette. On these lonely nights in King Hill before the trial, she "prayed I could have [Harriet Tubman's] kind of courage on the trial day."

Claudette and three other brave black women were chosen to testify in the lawsuit that sought for the courts to declare that Montgomery's and Alabama's transportation segregation was unconstitutional: a direct challenge not only to bus segregation but also the oppressive Southern way of life based on the unfair dictates of Jim Crow. A warm Friday May 11, 1956 was a special day at the Federal Court House in Montgomery on the 159th day of the Montgomery Bus Boycott, when the trial long-awaited finally began.

Here, Claudette testified with a calm confidence, relating how she was "very hurt [and] crying [when] the policeman said, 'I will have to take you off' [but] I didn't move [and] so he kicked me." After her testimony, "I was surrounded by adults [and] Everyone was shaking my hand [and that night] I looked over at Raymond, fast asleep in his bassinet, and I said, 'I think I might have done us some good today'."

At last, the Montgomery Bus Boycott ended on June 19, 1956. On this historic day, the fair-minded judges of the district court determined that state and city segregation, including on the city buses that now had to be fairly integrated in equality, against United States citizens was unconstitutional, because it violated the rights and liberties of United States citizens in the landmark case of *Browder v. Gayle*.

Of course, the key to this landmark legal case had been the testimony of four women, especially Claudette, the key plaintiff, who was the youngest. They had testified as part of a class-action lawsuit, revealing the extent of the anti-black discrimination and abuse on the city buses in the lawsuit against the segregation laws of Montgomery and Alabama on the premise that they were unconstitutional.

Claudette's testimony was all-important for the winning decision that brought a brighter day to blacks across the South. After all, she had longed for "a chance to speak out. I was still angry [and] I wanted white people to know that I wasn't satisfied with segregation. Black people, too."

Claudette's earlier personal decisions had been backed-up by the judges of the court—that state and city laws cannot take away the freedoms and rights, not only legal but also human rights in general, of United States citizens, because they were promised and guaranteed in the United States Constitution. Ironically, the judges verified the truth of Claudette's very words, which were repeated in frustrated desperation and with passion, when she had been arrested and dragged away by two white police officers like a common criminal on March 2, 1955: "It's my constitutional right!"

Most important with the final verdict in the winning of the trial that ended legal segregation, the famous Montgomery "bus boycott ignited by Claudette's arrest twenty-one months earlier came to an end. It was one of the great human rights victories" in the annals of United States history.

Indeed, as Claudette summarized the importance of the case and her own key role with the three other female plaintiffs: "It was the Browder v. Gaye case that [had] made the boycott a success [and] people should that there were four women that made the Montgomery Bus Boycott successful, which gave Dr. [Martin Luther] King notoriety. I wasn't seeking notoriety. But . . . the four women in the Supreme Court Case [should] be known" today, because of the importance of their timely and selfless contributions to the cause of human rights.

Enduring Legacies

However, because her bold actions which had fully revealed "that at least one young Alabaman would not share her future with Jim Crow" in dramatic fashion, Claudette had left an enduring moral and Civil Rights legacy that was all-important in many ways. As Gray emphasized: "the case gave me courage and a faith that there would be another opportunity to challenge Alabama's segregation laws" in the future.

As mentioned and in summary, the great opportunity had finally come in Browder v. Gayle, when "Claudette was one of the plaintiffs in that case [and] Claudette's [earlier act helped give Mrs. [Rosa] Parks [whose arrest for refusing to leave her bus seat on December 1, 1955 had been well-organized and preplanned, including by Gray, based on the earlie Claudette Colvin model] the moral courage to do what she later did."

Gray also admitted the real and most forgotten source of Rosa Park's brave stand against Jim Crow segregation lay in the fact that she had been emboldened and inspired by Claudette's defiant stand around nine months before: "she was encouraged to do what she did by action taken . . . earlier by Claudette Colvin."

In more emphatic terms, Gray concluded how "if Claudette Colvin had not done what she did on March 2, 1955, Mrs. Parks may never had done what she did no December 1, 1955."

After having accomplished all that she could in the name of justice and equality in Montgomery and succeeded in her own personal mission that was well done to have made Harriet Tubman immensely proud, Claudette left for New York City in 1958 to start a new life not long after the trial's end. Quite simply, she had outgrown Montgomery and sought greener pastures now that integration, greater equality, and a new day had come to Montgomery, as if mission accomplished.

Even more, Claudette needed to leave Montgomery and its searing racial memories also because of the unfortunate Jeremiah Reeves, who became the most tragic of victims. After having been framed and forced to confess to half a dozen rapes of white women that he never committed, Jeremiah lingered on death row for more than half a decade. Finally, on March 28, 1958, he was sent to the electric chair for the crimes that he never committed, but, of course, not in the eyes of an all-white jury and a white judge in Montgomery.

Ironically, the tragic life of Claudette's schoolmate and neighborhood friend came to an end on a sunny spring-like day in late March like when she had decided to make her own defiant stand against the injustice and discrimination of America's own Apartheid system. And this insidious system of oppression had been so harsh that even some leading Nazi's had rejected it as having been too severe for Germany against the Jewish people during the 1930s.

As Claudette explained about this tumultuous period of great change for the better in her life upon a satisfied reflection of having conducted her life in her own way and based on her own decisions: "I just went on my own, and I knew I had to take care of myself. I am a self-made Woman. You have to have strong courage, strong faith, and belief in yourself."

In the end, Claudette Colvin found a rewarding new life and professional career in an open and tolerant melting part of New York City, which was the antithesis of the oppressive life in Montgomery and the Deep South. Here, greater equality existed for all people, regardless of color and background.

For decades, she thrived in a professional career to fulfill a longtime dream, gaining nurse's training and becoming a respected nurse's aide. Claudette Colvin helped elderly people in need of care at a Catholic hospital for decades, succeeding in a personally reward profession and enjoying a fulfilling life.

In one of the great ironies, Claudette kept the secrets of her activist and protest past as an early Civil Rights pioneer to herself decade after decade because she was modest and shy, while enjoying keeping a low profile in busy New York City. Most of all, it was the comforting knowledge about what she had accomplished against the odds at Montgomery in dramatic fashion in the name of civil and human rights by playing a leading role in having destroyed the legal basis of for segregation, which provided a lifelong sense of inner peace and solace that brought Claudette a great deal of personal comfort.

As she summarized her significant contributions that finally helped to change the South forever: "those degrading signs, 'White' and 'Colored' are gone. We destroyed them. There are laws now that make segregation illegal. We forced white people to take a different view. They had to change their attitude toward blacks. The civil rights movement cleared the way legally so we could progress. It opened the doors for a younger generation. I'm glad I was a part of that."

As could be expected, Claudette was guilty of considerable understatement in her typical modest way. But in truth as emphasized by Civil Rights leaders and famous attorney Fred D. Gray, who wrote how: "She gave the moral courage . . . Dr. King [because] a 15-year-old girl who did what she did, and was willing to take whatever consequences, not knowing what as going to happen. When you compare it, Claudette had a lot more courage than many of us" at the time.

Epilogue

In the end, Claudette Colvin had remained true not only to herself but also to the sacred memory of Harriet Tubman, who she so admired and whose stirring legacy—like that of Sojourner Truth—had played such a key role in inspiring and determining her heroic actions on March 2, 1955. By loving history so passionately and admiring its heroines with such sincerity, Claudette became part of history in the end.

Indeed, this shy and serious-minded Alabama teenager became a distinguished heroine for a spirited defiance and courage demonstrated when on her own, which had been derived from heartfelt feelings and moral convictions that came from deep inside her soul.

In many ways and as she had sincerely believed, it almost seemed as if the ghost of Harriet Tubman and Sojourner Truth has been beside Claudette during her great showdown with evil. In her own words: "Living in a segregated society, I wasn't going out of my boundaries looking for trouble [because] I didn't have any support."

On that momentous day, March 2, 1955, that actually gave birth to the Montgomery Bus Boycott and the Civil Rights Movement, the words of Harriet Tubman still echoed in the heart and mind of Claudette Colvin, because they still applied to her own life and brave actions that helped to liberate an entire people from Jim Crow bondage, just like the legendary "Black Moses" had liberated so many of her people from permanent bondage during the antebellum period and the Civil War: "I did not take up this work for my own benefit, but for those of my race who need help"—a noble epitaph that also applied to the remarkable life of Claudette Colvin, who was a forgotten mother of the Civil Rights Movement.

Because fifteen-year-old Claudette Colvin could no longer tolerant the overwhelming extent of the racial injustices and indignities of Jim Crow and fully demonstrated as much on warm afternoon of March 2, 1955 and after having been supremely inspired by the courage of Harriet Tubman and other leading black heroes and heroines, Claudette had initiated a people's social revolution in the dark heart of the Deep South.

Most of all, Claudette had endlessly admired these bold black women—Harriet Tubman and Sojourner Truth—because they had bravely stood up and fought against the horrors of slavery and played roles in its destruction to bring a new day and birth of freedom to America in an unprecedented social and political revolution. In much the same way, Claudette Colvin had also ignited another political and social revolution that also changed America for the better.

In the words of her pastor that were no exaggeration, Reverend H. H. Johnson had emphasized not long thereafter her arrest how: "I think that you just brought the revolution to Montgomery."

Indeed, this prophetic vision for the long-awaited arrival of a bright, new day was no case of hyperbole expressed by the good reverend, who never lost his faith in Claudette, who had made her mark in the world while still in her teens.

But in the end, perhaps Fred D. Gray said it best: "if Claudette Colvin had not done what she did on March 2, 1955, Mrs. [Rosa] Parks may never had done what she did on December 1, 1955. If Mrs. Parks had given up her seat . . . . she would never have been arrested; there would never have been a trial on December 5, 1955; no beginning of the Montgomery Bus Boycott; no mass meeting at Holt Street Baptist Church and Dr. Martin Luther King Jr. would not have been introduced to the nation on December 5, 1955 [and] The whole history of the civil rights movement may have been different but for Claudette [because these stirring] events that occurred in Montgomery . . . not only changed the city of Montgomery, the state of Alabama, and these United States, but also changed the world . . . And it all started on a bus in Montgomery, Alabama," with the courageous defiance of a remarkable young woman named Claudette Colvin.

At age fifteen, Claudette had most of all admired the heroic memory and legacy of freedom fighter and liberator Harriet Tubman, and, as Colvin believed, they were side-by-side on a segregated Montgomery bus and fought against injustice together and as one on the historic afternoon of March 2, 1955.

About the Author

PHILLIP THOMAS TUCKER, Ph.D., has won international acclaim on both sides of the Atlantic as today's leading "New Look" historian, who has authored a large number of "New Look" books of unique distinction. Throughout his career as a professional historian, he has focused on a wide variety of unique aspects of the African American and Caribbean experience to reveal its full richness and complexities, while bestowing long-overdue recognition to forgotten men and women. Like his groundbreaking *Haitian Revolutionary Women Series* (3 volumes), the *New Look Glory 54th Massachusetts Series* (4 volumes) has continued the author's long-existing tradition of bestowing well-deserved recognition and praising the impressive achievements of remarkable African Americans, men and women, throughout the annals of American history. One of America's most prolific and groundbreaking historians, Tucker has authored more than nearly 70 highly-original books to reveal long-ignored and silenced chapters of history, while correcting the historical record for the twenty-first century.

Bibliography

Alabama Journal, Montgomery Alabama.

Bradford, Sarah, *Harriet Tubman, The Moses of Her People*, (Bedford: Appleton Books, 1993).

Braund, Kathryn E. Holland, editor, *Tohopeka, Rethinking the Creek and the War of 1812*, (Tuscaloosa: University of Alabama Press, 2012).

Churchill, Winston, *Memoirs of the Second World War*, (Boston: Houghton Mifflin Company, 1987).

Clinton, Catherine, *Harriet Tubman, The Road to Freedom*, (New York: Back Bay Books, 2005).

Dierenfield, Bruce J., *The Civil Rights Movement*, (Boca Raton: Routledge Publishers, 2008)

Gates, Henry Louis, Sr., *The African Americans, Many Rivers to Cross*, (Carlsbad: Smiley Books, 2013).

Gray, Fred D., *Bus Ride to Justice, The Life and Works of Fred D. Gray*, (Montgomery: New South Books, 2013).

House, Phillip, *Claudette Colvin, Twice Toward Justice*, (New York: Farrar Straus Giroux, 2009).

Montgomery Advertiser, Montgomery, Alabama.

Morris, Alden, *The Origins of the Civil Rights Movement, Communities Organizing for Change*, (New York: The Free Press, 1986).

Phibbs, Cheryl, *The Montgomery Bus Boycott, A History and Reference Guild*, (Westport: Greenwood Publishing, 2009)

Truth, Sojourner, *Narrative of Sojourner Truth*, (private printing, 2018).

Tucker, Phillip Thomas, *Harriet Tubman's Intense Religious Faith in Maryland, Genesis of an American Heroine and Icon*, (Portland: PublishNation, 2019).

Tucker, Phillip Thomas, *Be Free or Die! Harriet Tubman in Her Own Words, Inspirational Quotes of "Black Moses,"* (Portland: PublishNation, 2019).

Whitman, James Q., *Hitler's American Model, The United States and the Making of Nazi Race Law*, (Princeton: Princeton University Press, 2017).

United States City Guide, *Montgomery, Alabama, The Guide to the American City*, (United States City Guides, 2010).

25/1/22.

Claudette had her conviction quashed in November 2021.
60 odd years after her protest.
Heard her tonight on the world service @ 3.00 AM.

Printed in Great Britain
by Amazon